Back to Basics: Data Analysis

By Lillian Pierson, P.E.,
Meta S. Brown and Paul McFedries

WILEY

Publisher's Acknowledgments

Authors: Lillian Pierson, P.E., Meta S. Brown and Paul McFedries

Associate Publisher: Katie Mohr

Project Editor: Lynn Northrup

Editorial Assistant: Matthew Lowe

Production Editor: Magesh Elangovan

Cover Design: Wiley

Cover Images: (Magnifying Glass) ©lushik/Getty Images, (Data Funnel) ©da-vooda/Getty Images

Back to Basics: Data Analysis

Published by:
John Wiley & Sons, Inc.,
111 River Street,
Hoboken, NJ 07030-5774,
www.wiley.com

For general information on our other products and services, please contact our Customer Care Department within the U.S. at 877-762-2974, outside the U.S. at 317-572-3993, or fax 317-572-4002.

Library of Congress Control Number: 2019945383

ISBN 978-1-119-61162-2

Manufactured in the United States of America

F10012472_072619

Table of Contents

1

Introducing Data Analysis

For quite some time now, *everyone* has been absolutely deluged by data. It's coming from every computer, every mobile device, every camera, and every imaginable sensor — and now it's even coming from watches and other wearable technologies. Data is generated in every social media interaction we make, every file we save, every picture we take, and every query we submit; it's even generated when we do something as simple as ask a favorite search engine for directions to the closest ice-cream shop.

You may have wondered, "What's the point of all this data? Why use valuable resources to generate and collect it?" Although even a single decade ago, no one was in a position to make much use of most of the data that's generated, the tides today have definitely turned. Specialists known as *data engineers* are constantly finding innovative and powerful new ways to capture, collate, and condense unimaginably massive volumes of data, and other specialists, known as *data analysts*, are leading change by deriving valuable and actionable insights from that data.

In its truest form, data analysis represents the optimization of processes and resources. Data analysis produces *data insights* — actionable, data-informed conclusions or predictions that you can use to understand and improve your business, your investments, your health, and even your lifestyle and social life. Using data analysis insights is like being able to see in the dark. For any goal or pursuit you can imagine, you can find data analysis methods to help you predict the most direct route from where you are to where you want to be — and to anticipate every pothole in the road between both places.

Understand the Components of Data Analysis

To practice data analysis, in the true meaning of the term, you need the analytical know-how of math and statistics, the coding skills necessary to work with data, and an area of subject matter expertise. Without this expertise, you might as well call yourself a mathematician or a statistician. Similarly, a software programmer without subject matter expertise and analytical know-how might better be considered a software engineer or developer, but not a data analyst.

Because the demand for data insights is increasing exponentially, every area is forced to adopt data analysis. As such, different flavors of data analysis have emerged. The following are just a few titles under which experts of every discipline are using data analysis: ad tech data analyst, director of banking digital analyst, clinical data analyst, geoengineer data analyst, geospatial analytics data analyst, political analyst, retail personalization data analyst, and clinical informatics analyst in pharmacometrics. Given that it often seems that no one without a scorecard can keep track of who's a data analyst, in the following sections I spell out the key components that are part of any data analysis role.

Collect, query, and consume data

Data engineers have the job of capturing and collating large volumes of structured, unstructured, and semi-structured *big data* — data that exceeds the processing capacity of conventional database systems because it's too big, it moves too fast, or it doesn't fit the structural requirements of traditional database architectures. Again, data engineering tasks are separate from the work that's performed in data analysis, which focuses more on insight, prediction, and visualization. Despite this distinction, whenever data analysts collect, query, and consume data during the analysis process, they perform work similar to that of the data engineer.

Although valuable insights can be generated from a single data source, often the combination of several relevant sources delivers the contextual information required to drive better data-informed decisions. A data analyst can work from several datasets that are stored in a single database, or even in several different data warehouses. At other times, source data is stored and processed on a cloud-based platform that's been built by software and data engineers.

No matter how the data is combined or where it's stored, if you're a data analyst, you almost always have to *query* data — write commands to extract relevant datasets from data storage systems, in other words. Most of the time, you use Structured Query Language (SQL) to query data.

Whether you're using an application or doing custom analyses by using a programming language such as R or Python, you can choose from a number of universally accepted file formats:

- **Comma-separated values (CSV) files:** Almost every brand of desktop and web-based analysis application accepts this file type, as do commonly used scripting languages such as Python and R.
- **Scripts:** Most data analysts know how to use either the Python or R programming language to analyze and visualize data. These script files end with the extension .py or .ipynb (Python) or .r (R).

- **Application files:** Excel is useful for quick-and-easy, spot-check analyses on small- to medium-size datasets. These application files have the .xls or .xlsx extension. Geospatial analysis applications such as ArcGIS and QGIS save with their own proprietary file formats (the .mxd extension for ArcGIS and the .qgs extension for QGIS).
- **Web programming files:** If you're building custom, web-based data visualizations, you may be working in D3.js — or Data-Driven Documents, a JavaScript library for data visualization. When you work in D3.js, you use data to manipulate web-based documents using .html, .svg, and .css files.

Apply mathematical modeling to data analysis tasks

Data analysis relies heavily on a practitioner's math skills (and statistics skills, as described in the following section) precisely because these are the skills needed to understand your data and its significance. These skills are also valuable in data analysis because you can use them to carry out predictive forecasting, decision modeling, and hypotheses testing.

Keep in mind that *mathematics* uses deterministic methods to form a *quantitative* (or *numerical*) description of the world; *statistics* is a form of science that's derived from mathematics, but it focuses on using a *stochastic* (probabilities) approach and inferential methods to form a quantitative description of the world. For more on descriptive and inferential statistics, see Chapter 7.

Data analysts use mathematical methods to build decision models, generate approximations, and make predictions about the future. Chapter 7 presents many complex applied mathematical approaches that are useful when working in data analysis.

Derive insights from statistical methods

In data analysis, statistical methods are useful for better understanding your data's significance, for validating hypotheses, for simulating scenarios, and for making predictive forecasts of future events. Advanced statistical skills are somewhat rare, even among quantitative analysts, engineers, and scientists. If you want to go places in data analysis, though, take some time to get up to speed in a few basic statistical methods, like linear and logistic regression, naïve Bayes classification, and time series analysis. These methods are covered in Chapter 7.

Play the coding game

Coding is unavoidable when you're working in data analysis. You need to be able to write code so that you can instruct the computer how you want it to manipulate, analyze, and visualize your data. Programming languages such as R and

Python are important for writing scripts for data manipulation, analysis, and visualization, and SQL is useful for data querying. The JavaScript library D3.js is a hot new option for making cool, custom, and interactive web-based data visualizations.

Although coding is a requirement for data analysis, it doesn't have to be this big scary *thing* that people make it out to be. Your coding can be as fancy and complex as you want it to be, but you can also take a rather simple approach. Although these skills are paramount to success, you can learn enough coding to practice high-level data analysis.

Apply data analysis to a subject area

Statisticians have exhibited some measure of obstinacy in accepting the significance of data analysis. Many statisticians have cried out, "Data analysis is nothing new! It's just another name for what we've been doing all along." However, the main point of distinction between statistics and data analysis is the need for subject matter expertise.

Because statisticians usually have only a limited amount of expertise in fields outside of statistics, they're almost always forced to consult with a subject matter expert to verify exactly what their findings mean and to decide the best direction in which to proceed. Data analysts, on the other hand, are required to have a strong subject matter expertise in the area in which they're working. Data analysts generate deep insights and then use their domain-specific expertise to understand exactly what those insights mean with respect to the area in which they're working.

This list describes a few ways in which subject matter experts are using data analysis to enhance performance in their respective industries:

- **Engineers** use machine learning to optimize energy efficiency in modern building design.
- **Clinical data analysts** work on the personalization of treatment plans and use healthcare informatics to predict and preempt future health problems in at-risk patients.
- **Marketing data analysts** use logistic regression to predict and preempt *customer churn* (the loss of customers from a product or service to that of a competitor's).
- **Data journalists** *scrape* websites (extract data in-bulk directly off the pages on a website, in other words) for fresh data in order to discover and report the latest breaking-news stories.
- **Data analysts in crime analysis** use spatial predictive modeling to predict, preempt, and prevent criminal activities.
- **Data do-gooders** use machine learning to classify and report vital information about disaster-affected communities for real-time decision support in humanitarian response.

Communicate data insights

As a data analyst, you must have sharp oral and written communication skills. If a data analyst can't communicate, all the knowledge and insight in the world does *nothing* for your organization. Data analysts need to be able to explain data insights in a way that staff members can understand. Not only that, data analysts need to be able to produce clear and meaningful data visualizations and written narratives. Most of the time, people need to see something for themselves in order to understand. Data analysts must be creative and pragmatic in their means and methods of communication.

Who Can Use Data Analysis?

The terms *data analysis* and *data engineering* are often misused and confused, so let me start off by clarifying that these two fields are, in fact, separate and distinct domains of expertise. *Data analysis* is the computational science of extracting meaningful insights from raw data and then effectively communicating those insights to generate value. *Data engineering,* on the other hand, is an engineering domain that's dedicated to building and maintaining systems that overcome data-processing bottlenecks and data-handling problems for applications that consume, process, and store large volumes, varieties, and velocities of data. In both data analysis and data engineering, you commonly work with these three data varieties:

- **Structured:** Data is stored, processed, and manipulated in a traditional relational database management system (RDBMS).
- **Unstructured:** Data is commonly generated from human activities and doesn't fit into a structured database format.
- **Semi-structured:** Data doesn't fit into a structured database system, but is nonetheless structured by tags that are useful for creating a form of order and hierarchy in the data.

A lot of people believe that only large organizations that have massive funding are implementing data analysis methodologies to optimize and improve their business, but that's not the case. The proliferation of data has created a demand for insights, and this demand is embedded in many aspects of our modern culture — from the Uber passenger who expects his driver to pick him up exactly at the time and location predicted by the Uber application, to the online shopper who expects the Amazon platform to recommend the best product alternatives so she can compare similar goods before making a purchase. Data and the need for data-informed insights are ubiquitous. Because organizations of all sizes are beginning to recognize that they're immersed in a sink-or-swim, data-driven, competitive environment, data know-how emerges as a core and requisite function in almost every line of business.

What does this mean for the everyday person? First, it means that everyday employees are increasingly expected to support a progressively advancing set of technological requirements. Why? Because almost all industries are becoming increasingly reliant on data technologies and the insights they generate. Consequently, many people are in continual need of upgrading their tech skills, or else they face the real possibility of being replaced by a more tech-savvy employee.

The good news is that upgrading tech skills doesn't usually require people to go back to college, or get a university degree in statistics, computer science, or data analysis. The bad news is that, even with professional training or self-teaching, it always takes extra work to stay industry-relevant and tech-savvy. In this respect, the data revolution isn't so different from any other change that has hit industry in the past. The fact is, in order to stay relevant, you need to take the time and effort to acquire only the skills that keep you current. When you're learning how to do data analysis, you can take some courses, educate yourself using online resources, read books like this one, and attend events where you can learn what you need to know to stay on top of the game.

Who can use data analysis? You can. Your organization can. Your employer can. Anyone who has a bit of understanding and training can begin using data insights to improve their lives, their careers, and the bottom line of their businesses.

Data analysis represents a change in the way you approach the world. When predicting outcomes, people often used to make their best guess, act, and then hope for their desired result. With data insights, however, people now have access to the predictive vision that they need to truly drive change and achieve the results they need.

You can use data insights to bring about changes in the following areas:

- **Business systems:** Optimize returns on investment for any measurable activity.
- **Technical marketing strategy development:** Use data insights and predictive analytics to identify marketing strategies that work, eliminate under-performing efforts, and test new marketing strategies.
- **Keep communities safe:** Predictive policing applications help law enforcement personnel predict and prevent local criminal activities.
- **Help make the world a better place for those less fortunate:** Data analysts in developing nations are using social data, mobile data, and data from websites to generate real-time analytics that improve the effectiveness of humanitarian response to disaster, epidemics, food scarcity issues, and more.

Examine Data Analysis Solutions

Organizations and their leaders are still grappling with how to best use big data and data analysis. Most of them know that advanced analytics is positioned to bring a tremendous competitive edge to their organizations, but few of them have any idea about the options that are available or the exact benefits that data analysis can deliver. In this section, I introduce three major data analysis solution alternatives and describe the benefits that a data analysis implementation can deliver.

Assemble your own in-house team

Many organizations find it makes financial sense for them to establish their own dedicated in-house team of data professionals. This saves them money they would otherwise spend achieving similar results by hiring independent consultants or deploying a ready-made cloud-based analytics solution. Three options for building an in-house data analysis team are:

- **Train existing employees.** If you want to equip your organization with the power of data analysis and analytics, data analysis training (the lower-cost alternative) can transform existing staff into data-skilled, highly specialized subject matter experts for your in-house team.

- **Hire trained personnel.** Some organizations fill their requirements by either hiring experienced data analysts or by hiring fresh data analysis graduates. The problem with this approach is that there aren't enough of these people to go around, and if you do find people who are willing to come onboard, they have high salary requirements. Remember, in addition to the math, statistics, and coding requirements, data analysts must have a high level of subject matter expertise in the specific field where they're working. That's why it's extraordinarily difficult to find these individuals. Until universities make data literacy an integral part of every educational program, finding highly specialized and skilled data analysts to satisfy organizational requirements will be nearly impossible.
- **Train existing employees and hire some experts.** A third, and possibly the best, option is to train existing employees to do high-level data analysis tasks and then bring on a few experienced data analysts to fulfill your more advanced data analysis problem-solving and strategy requirements.

Outsource requirements to private data analysis consultants

Many organizations prefer to outsource their data analysis and analytics requirements to an outside expert, using one of two general strategies:

- **Comprehensive:** This strategy serves the entire organization. To build an advanced data analysis implementation for your organization, you can hire a private consultant to help you with a comprehensive strategy development. This type of service will likely cost you, but you can receive tremendously valuable insights in return. A strategist will know about the options available to meet your requirements, as well as the benefits and drawbacks of each one. With a strategy in hand and an on-call expert available to help you, you can much more easily navigate the task of building an internal team.
- **Individual:** You can apply piecemeal solutions to specific problems that arise, or that have arisen, within your organization. If you're not prepared for the rather involved process of comprehensive strategy design and implementation, you can contract out smaller portions of work to a private data analysis consultant. This spot-treatment approach could still deliver the benefits of data analysis without requiring you to

reorganize the structure and financials of your entire organization.

Leverage cloud-based platform solutions

A cloud-based solution can deliver the power of data analytics to professionals who have only a modest level of data literacy. Some have seen the explosion of big data and data analysis coming from a long way off. Although it's still new to most, professionals and organizations in the know have been working fast and furiously to prepare. New, private cloud applications such as Trusted Analytics Platform, or TAP (`http://trustedanalytics.org`), are dedicated to making it easier and faster for organizations to deploy their big data initiatives. Other cloud services, like Tableau, offer code-free, automated data services — from basic clean-up and statistical modeling to analysis and data visualization. Though you still need to understand the statistical, mathematical, and substantive relevance of the data insights, applications such as Tableau can deliver powerful results without requiring users to know how to write code or scripts.

If you decide to use cloud-based platform solutions to help your organization reach its data analysis objectives, keep in mind you still need in-house staff who are trained and skilled to design, run, and interpret the quantitative results from these platforms. The platform will not do away with the need for in-house training and data analysis expertise — it will merely augment your organization so that it can more readily achieve its objectives.

Explore Data Analysis as a Career Path

Throughout this book, I hope to show you the power of data analysis and how you can use that power to more quickly reach your personal and professional goals. No matter the sector in which you work, acquiring data analysis skills can transform you into a more marketable professional. The following list describes just a few key industry sectors that can benefit from data analysis and analytics:

- **Corporations, small- and medium-size enterprises (SMEs), and e-commerce businesses:** Production-costs optimization, sales maximization, marketing ROI increases, staff-productivity optimization, customer-churn reduction, customer lifetime-value increases, inventory requirements and sales predictions, pricing model optimization, fraud detection, collaborative filtering, recommendation engines, and logistics improvements

- **Governments:** Business-process and staff-productivity optimization, management decision-support enhancements, finance and budget forecasting, expenditure tracking and optimization, and fraud detection
- **Academia:** Resource-allocation improvements, student performance-management improvements, dropout reductions, business process optimization, finance and budget forecasting, and recruitment ROI increases

2

Data Analysis and Your Business

Saying that data analysts explore data in search of valuable patterns may create a mental image that's a bit magical or mysterious. You are about to replace that image with one that is far more down to earth and approachable. Data analysis is not magical, and its purpose is to eliminate mystery, a little bit at a time, from your business.

Understand Your Business Goals

You might explore a shopping mall or a quaint little town just for the experience of looking around, but when you're in data analysis, you're exploring with a specific purpose. The very first thing you'll do in any data analysis project will be to get a clear understanding of that purpose. As you work with data, you will frequently revisit your goals and give thought to whether and how the information you find within the data supports them, but your first priority must always be to address the business goals established at the start of the project.

When you're presented with a goal, always discuss and document success criteria from the start. Although you may only be responsible for a narrow part of the work needed to achieve the business goal, understanding how the ultimate results will be evaluated helps you to understand the best ways to contribute to the project's success.

These success criteria may sound simple, but if you have doubts, you need to ask some questions. What kinds of questions? Let's look at an example.

Consider a data analysis project to help a local planning council. The council's mission is to promote economic well-being by encouraging land use that makes the community attractive to businesses and residents. A key part of its work is retaining and attracting businesses that employ local residents and offer good compensation. The council's business goal is to identify parcels of land that are about to change ownership, and to do so early enough to influence the use of the land.

Here are some questions you might ask:

- **Does the council expect that just one model will work for all types of property?** Industrial, commercial, single-family, multifamily, and so on — it's not realistic to think that you'll find one big equation to address them all.
- **How many property types exist?** You could have dozens.
- **Is the council equally interested in all properties?** You'd think large, industrial parcels would be the most important.
- **Which property types are most important to the council?** You may want to push for modeling just one or two important categories on the first round.

TIP Always ask about recent mishaps. Unspoken goals often include not repeating something that just went wrong.

Asking questions helps you to get more information, of course, but your questions do more than that. They help others on the team (including executives, if you have the opportunity to meet with them) become aware of what's missing, what's going to be challenging, and what's a lot more complicated than they thought it would be. By asking probing questions in the business-understanding phase, you help everyone to clarify thinking, define reasonable goals, and set realistic expectations. Then, based on the business goals, you define your data analysis goals.

It's important to remember that business goals are determined by the client (external or internal), not the data analyst. If you and your team have doubts about a particular goal, don't change it on your own. Clients won't accept that! Instead, enter into a discussion with the client, explain your concerns, and come to an agreement about reasonable business goals for the project.

You'll complete the phase of understanding your business goals by outlining your step-by-step action plan for completing the work (including a schedule and details of resources required for each step) and your initial assessment of the appropriate tools and techniques for the project.

Understand Your Data

In the data-understanding phase, you will first gather and broadly describe your data. The data-gathering process might involve assembling one or more datasets for you to use, possibly drawn from data used in earlier projects, as well as additional fields that you will need. Then you'll examine the data in a little more depth, exploring the data one variable (field) at a time, checking for consistency with expectations and any obvious signs of data quality problems.

You begin to review the data, making notes for your report as you work.

Describe the data

Your first concern is to identify the variables in each file and confirm that you have adequate documentation for each of them. You review each variable in the data, comparing the variable names to the information in the documentation.

You note findings about the data and the documentation, including the following:

- Whether most of the fields appear consistent with the documentation that you have
- Whether some of the fields in the data files are not explained in the documentation
- Whether some of the fields described in the documentation don't appear in the data

You write detailed notes about each file and each variable. Using your notes as a reference, you look for information to address the discrepancies. For example, you might find that

- A few of the fields in the data from public sources simply don't match the documentation provided (public data isn't always accurate or complete data).
- Additional notes are available to explain how some of the derived fields were created.
- Some of the undocumented data was obtained by *web scraping* (using specialized software to automatically extract information from websites), and you can't find any dependable documentation for it.

You update your notes about the data, revising them with additional documentation. You note which variables are still undocumented. Although some of those fields seem likely to have predictive value, a number of disadvantages exist to using them for predictive modeling, including the following:

- Some of the data was collected by web scraping. You're not confident that you'll be able to get that data in the future.
- You don't have details on the scraping process, so you can't be sure that scraped data was defined consistently.
- You'll have a hard time explaining the meaning of data without documentation.

So you decide that on the first attempt to develop a predictive model for property ownership change, you'll use only those fields that have been adequately documented. In a future project, you may seek out alternative sources for some of the other fields.

Explore the data

Now it's time to briefly examine the data for each variable in each file. You must check basics, such as whether the data is string or numeric, that the range of values is appropriate, and that the distribution of values looks reasonable. You'll note any discrepancies from the documentation and your own reasonable expectations.

For each field, you prepare a brief summary, with a name and description, number of missing cases, and the range of values (low and high). You may also include additional information such as a distribution graph, the average (mean), and most frequently occurring (mode) value of the variable. At this point, you won't try to relate one variable to another.

You start by using software (such as a spreadsheet program) that produces a basic report for each variable in the data, including information such as the range of values, the average for continuous variables, the most common value for categorical variables, and so on. This report is a starting point for understanding your data. You use it to identify what data you have and whether the data is consistent with what you were led to expect by the documentation and your colleagues. You add to it by using graphs or other simple methods for adding detail to your understanding of each variable.

As you review each variable, you describe it and make note of any concerns and what should be done to address them. In your summaries, you state whether the variable appears ready for use in modeling, needs further preparation, or is in such poor condition that it cannot be used.

Clean the data

You've explored the data and found that some of the fields that seem to have value for modeling exhibit minor errors or other issues that you want to correct first.

You go through each of the fields that you've found to be potentially useful, but not in perfect condition. As you work, you document your observations and any changes that you make. For each field, you judge whether it is good enough to use in modeling. (You're not deciding whether the variable will be in the final model or work well as a predictor, just whether it is of sufficient quality to test.) Finally, you combine your notes on these observations and actions into a data quality report.

Prepare Your Data

Now that you've gathered data and reviewed the fields one by one to familiarize yourself with the data and check for quality problems, you move forward and prepare the data for modeling. In this phase of your work, you do the necessary tasks to transform the data from its original form into the form you require for modeling, such as

- Joining datasets
- Specifying the roles of the fields
- Sampling the data
- Splitting your sample into subsets for building and testing models

Many projects call for deriving new fields based on the ones that are already in the data. For example, if the data has a field that contains both first and last names, your project might need to work with separate first and last names, so you'll need two new fields: one for the first name and one for the last name.

Import the data

In the data-understanding phase, you identified a number of fields that you won't use for modeling. You have ruled each of them out for one of these reasons:

- **Does not make sense as a predictor:** Includes unique fields such as an address or names, or something that you believe has no relationship to ownership change

- **Data quality is poor:** Many missing cases or incorrect values
- **Does not vary:** All cases have the same value (not necessarily a data quality problem)

You work with specialized data analysis software. Although you can do any of the same operations with other kinds of tools, your data analysis software is designed to help you view the steps of your process easily, and work quickly, by stringing together a sequence of operations represented by small icons. Each icon is a tool with a specific function and its own options and settings. This is called a *visual programming* interface.

If the data file is fairly large, you will import the data file into your database software of choice, remove the variables you cannot use, and save the rest in a new (somewhat smaller) file.

Derive new variables

Data management software does a lot of work for you, but there is no substitute for your business knowledge. You understand that, say, one variable represents the price paid for a property; another, the investments to improve the property;

and a third, the assessed value — but the software doesn't. The software only sees numbers and categories and text, not meaning. You understand that you have something of special interest about the relationships among those three variables, apart from any others. The software doesn't. You integrate this kind of business knowledge into your analysis by using it to derive appropriate new variables for modeling.

Split the data

Some of the machine learning techniques that are widely used in data analysis, such as decision trees and neural networks, call for one last bit of data preparation before constructing a model.

Data analysts can't always use theory to find one best model from data, as classical statisticians do. So, data analysts evaluate models by testing, testing, and testing. Some of the testing is hidden within the model-fitting process, automatic and (almost) unnoticed as you work. Some testing is done in the field through small-scale or full-scale deployment. And some of it is done by splitting off a portion of the data (called *test* or *holdout* data) before modeling and using your model to predict results for that data so that you can compare those predictions with what actually happened.

Model Your Data

Predictive models are nothing more than equations that help you make educated guesses in methodical, consistent ways, based on data.

People make predictions informally all the time, at home and at work:

- **Buying groceries:** Estimating consumption based on recent experience and anticipated changes, such as guests in the house or upcoming travel
- **Budgeting:** Planning for financial needs using information such as past spending, known upcoming events, and estimated requirements for emergency funds
- **Sales forecasting:** Anticipating future sales based on historical performance, envisioned deals, attitudes about the economy, and perhaps just a bit of wishful thinking

Because these informal predictions are made in an inconsistent, undocumented, and subjective way, it's hard to improve them. As a data analyst, you create dependable fact-based predictive models, and you document the process so that you can update and improve your models in the future.

Evaluate Your Results

Now that you've created a model, it's time to look the model over, see how it performs, and choose your next steps.

Your data analysis goal was to demonstrate the feasibility of using predictive modeling for property change ownership by showing that at least one variable has measurable predictive value for that purpose. Strictly speaking, you've met the goal, but if you still have time available before your deadline, you should use that time to improve on what you've done.

You have accomplished the minimum that you set out to provide. But you don't want to do just the minimum, so you keep working. You can try these things:

- Go back and do the data preparation needed for more of the model's factors.
- Experiment with alternative model types.
- Refine the model settings.

You document what you've accomplished so far, and then return to the work to build the best model that you can before the project due date.

3

Prepare Data for Analysis

As a data analyst, you will devote most of your time to preparation. Your effort will be rewarded, because good data preparation lays the groundwork for excellent data analysis results.

Data preparation takes time and patience. Many people spend much more time than necessary to do their data preparation, or get poor results, because they have never had the patience to devote time to mastering data analysis skills. Poor data preparation skills can cause failure to build an effective predictive model (perhaps while your competitor succeeds) and waste hours, even days, of valuable time on each project.

This chapter introduces a wide range of data manipulation methods that data analysts use to prepare data for modeling.

It's important that you become familiar with all these so that you will know what to look for within your data analysis applications, and why.

Rearrange Data

Before you build models or do calculations of any type, you should arrange the data to make your work as easy as possible. You can control data format, display, and the way that data will be treated in your analysis.

Control variable order

The order of variables (columns) in a dataset is usually a matter of how they were arranged in the source file or the database query that was used to import them. That arrangement may not be convenient for you. If you have many variables, it may be hard to spot the ones you want to see. Or perhaps some order makes sense to you, and you'd like the variables arranged that way.

Data analysis applications often allow you to change the order of variables, but instructions rarely show up clearly in the menu or help. These functions are usually buried within tools that serve broader purposes. Look for subtle options like these within data viewers and dialog boxes for other procedures (especially those for data manipulation and data export):

- **Drag and drop:** Tables that display data or *metadata* (such as variable names and formats) may be interactive, allowing you to change variable order by dragging and dropping columns.
- **Up and Down buttons:** Buttons labeled with the word *Up* or *Down,* or arrows pointing up or down, let you move variables up or down within lists to change order. Both types are shown in Figure 3-1.
- **Selection order:** When you select variables from a list (as you would to use only a few of a dataset's variables in a particular procedure), the order in which you select them may persist in subsequent operations.
- **Sort gestures:** When viewing variable lists (metadata), you may have sort options that enable you to rearrange variables, perhaps in alphabetical order or by type.

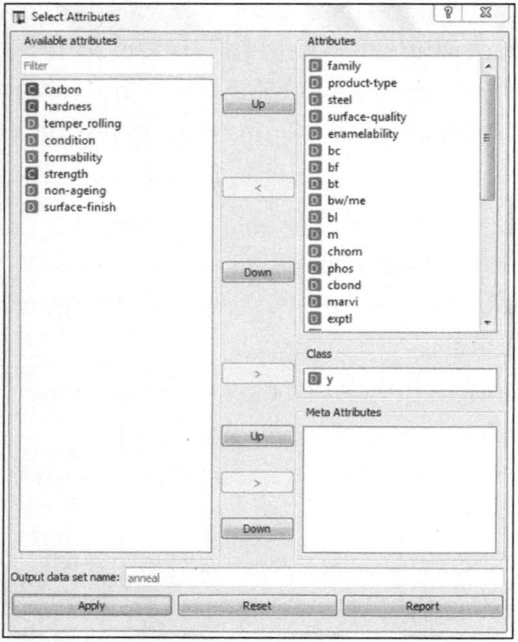

Figure 3-1: *Up and Down buttons let you change variable order.*

Format data properly

When you see a list of ZIP codes, you don't try to add or subtract them. You know that they represent places. You understand this because you have lots of experience seeing and recognizing ZIP codes.

Humans use experience when they interpret the data they see, but computers can't. Your data analysis software will do its best to identify the kind of data in each column, but data types are often ambiguous. So, it might interpret a ZIP code as an integer or continuous measure. In the end, it's up to you to define the proper format.

Functions for setting data formats and roles (such as denoting the dependent variable for modeling) can be buried within a variety of places in your data analysis application. You might define the formats and role of variables within a data file before you even open a data analysis application (the native data formats for Orange and Weka allow this), as part of the import (see Figure 3-2) or sometime later in the process. You may have tools built for this purpose, like the tools shown in Figures 3-3 and 3-4, or you may define these properties within other procedures.

Label data

Say, for example, you have a geographic region variable with four possible values: *East*, *West*, *North*, and *South*. You could store the information as strings, the full words typed out, or in a shorter code, such as 1 for East, 2 for West, and so on. Using the code reduces data entry time, prevents errors, and reduces the memory requirements for storing the data. But the codes are meaningless unless you have documentation, or *labels*, to explain their meaning.

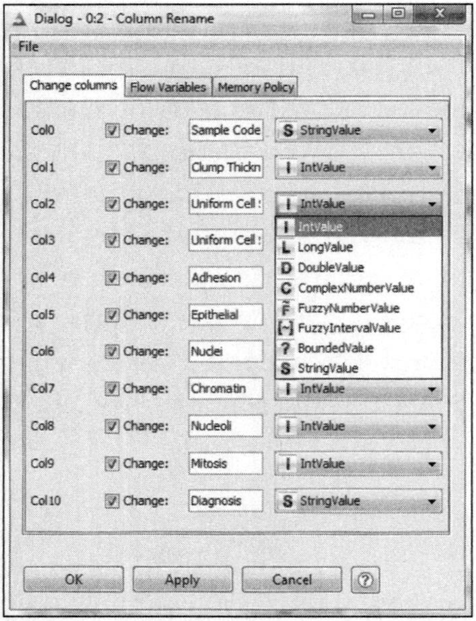

Figure 3-2: *Name and format change within a data import tool.*

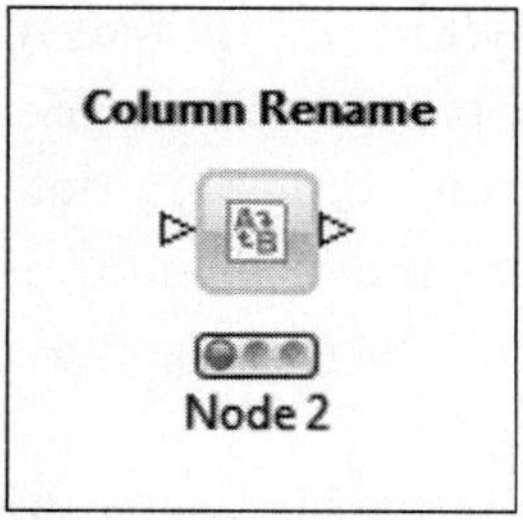

Figure 3-3: *This tool is devoted to changing variable names.*

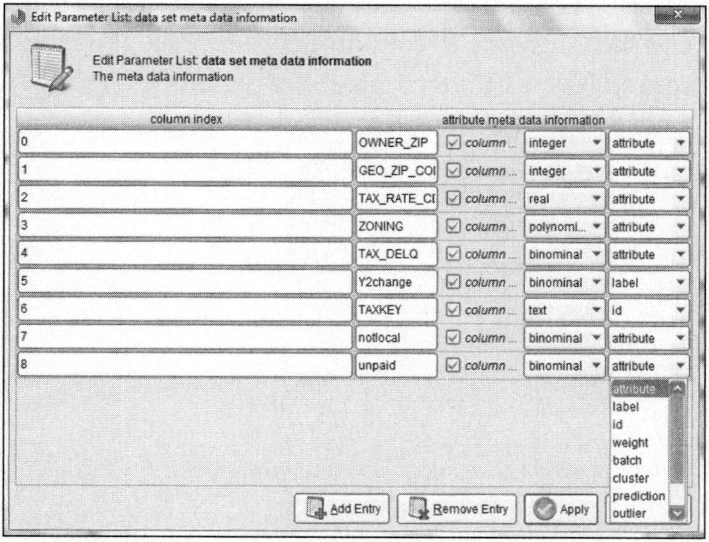

Figure 3-4: *Role options within a name change tool.*

Some data formats enable you to enjoy the advantages of using codes while keeping the information about the meaning of the codes in the same file. These aren't typical in data analysis — you're more likely to see them in statistical analysis products — but some data analysis applications can use these labeled data formats. Here's how they work.

Consider Figure 3-5, which shows a dataset open in the PSPP statistical analysis application. (If you'd like to experiment with PSPP, you can find it at `www.gnu.org/software/pspp`.) The data appears to contain only numbers, but these numbers are codes for values of categorical variables. Figure 3-6

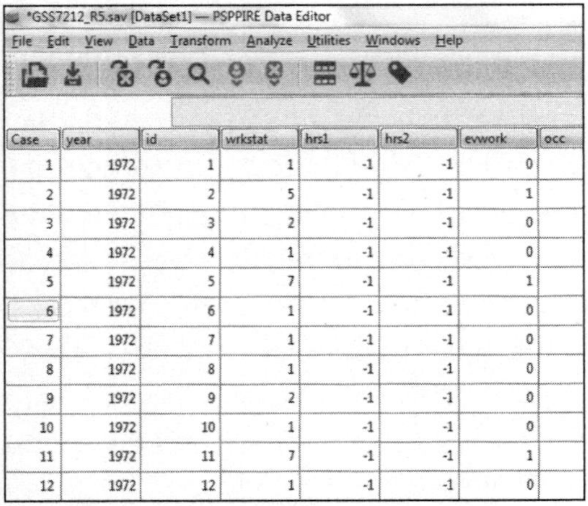

Case	year	id	wrkstat	hrs1	hrs2	evwork	occ
1	1972	1	1	-1	-1	0	
2	1972	2	5	-1	-1	1	
3	1972	3	2	-1	-1	0	
4	1972	4	1	-1	-1	0	
5	1972	5	7	-1	-1	1	
6	1972	6	1	-1	-1	0	
7	1972	7	1	-1	-1	0	
8	1972	8	1	-1	-1	0	
9	1972	9	2	-1	-1	0	
10	1972	10	1	-1	-1	0	
11	1972	11	7	-1	-1	1	
12	1972	12	1	-1	-1	0	

Figure 3-5: *Unlabeled data values.*

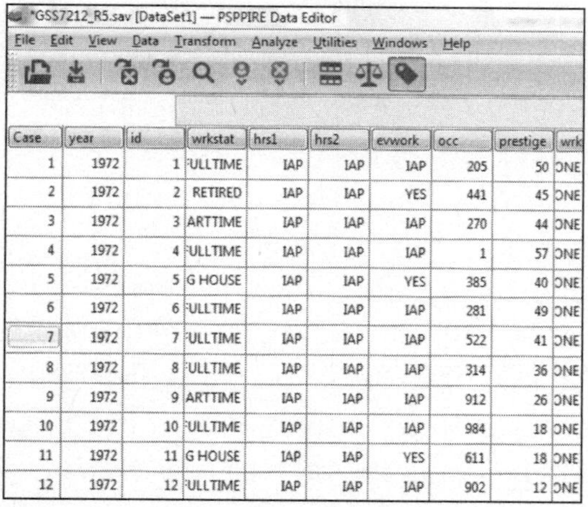

Case	year	id	wrkstat	hrs1	hrs2	evwork	occ	prestige	wrk
1	1972	1	ULLTIME	IAP	IAP	IAP	205	50	ONE
2	1972	2	RETIRED	IAP	IAP	YES	441	45	ONE
3	1972	3	ARTTIME	IAP	IAP	IAP	270	44	ONE
4	1972	4	ULLTIME	IAP	IAP	IAP	1	57	ONE
5	1972	5	G HOUSE	IAP	IAP	YES	385	40	ONE
6	1972	6	ULLTIME	IAP	IAP	IAP	281	49	ONE
7	1972	7	ULLTIME	IAP	IAP	IAP	522	41	ONE
8	1972	8	ULLTIME	IAP	IAP	IAP	314	36	ONE
9	1972	9	ARTTIME	IAP	IAP	IAP	912	26	ONE
10	1972	10	ULLTIME	IAP	IAP	IAP	984	18	ONE
11	1972	11	G HOUSE	IAP	IAP	YES	611	18	ONE
12	1972	12	ULLTIME	IAP	IAP	IAP	902	12	ONE

Figure 3-6: *The same data values shown as labels.*

shows the same dataset with labels instead of numeric codes. You can switch back and forth between these two display options using the menu, as shown in Figure 3-7. Although the data is stored as numbers, the labels allow you to see what the data means, whether you are looking at it in the data editor, as in Figure 3-6, setting up an analysis, or viewing the results.

You may also find other types of data labels in data analysis applications. The native data format for Weka allows you to include comments in a dataset (see Figure 3-8); this gives you

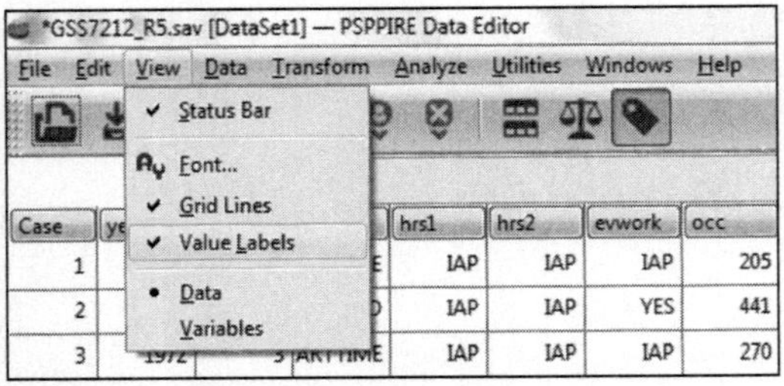

Figure 3-7: *Switching between display options.*

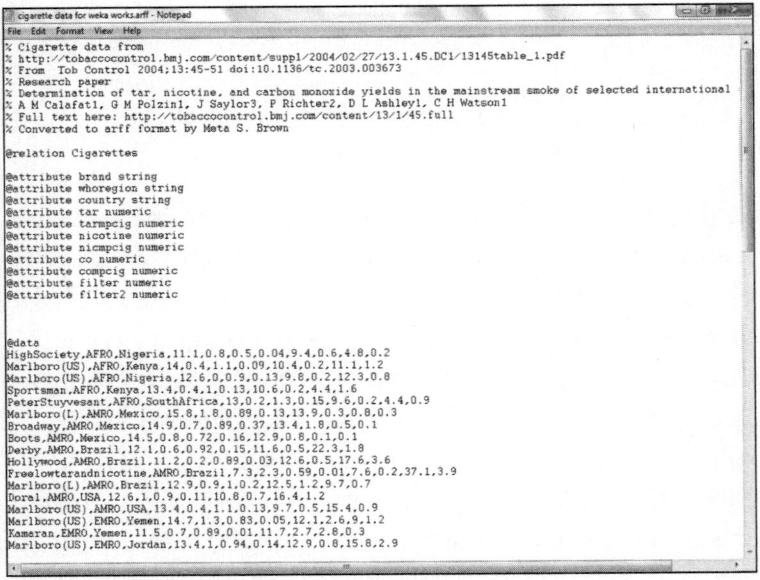

```
% Cigarette data from
% http://tobaccocontrol.bmj.com/content/suppl/2004/02/27/13.1.45.DC1/13145table_1.pdf
% From  Tob Control 2004;13:45-51 doi:10.1136/tc.2003.003673
% Research paper
% Determination of tar, nicotine, and carbon monoxide yields in the mainstream smoke of selected international
% A M Calafat1, G M Polzin1, J Saylor3, P Richter2, D L Ashley1, C H Watson1
% Full text here: http://tobaccocontrol.bmj.com/content/13/1/45.full
% Converted to arff format by Meta S. Brown

@relation Cigarettes

@attribute brand string
@attribute whoregion string
@attribute country string
@attribute tar numeric
@attribute tarmpcig numeric
@attribute nicotine numeric
@attribute nicmpcig numeric
@attribute co numeric
@attribute compcig numeric
@attribute filter numeric
@attribute filter2 numeric



@data
HighSociety,AFRO,Nigeria,11.1,0.8,0.5,0.04,9.4,0.6,4.8,0.2
Marlboro(US),AFRO,Kenya,14,0.4,1.1,0.09,10.4,0.2,11.1,1.2
Marlboro(US),AFRO,Nigeria,12.6,0,0.9,0.13,9.8,0.2,12.3,0.8
Sportsman,AFRO,Kenya,13.4,0.4,1,0.13,10.6,0.2,4.4,1.6
PeterStuyvesant,AFRO,SouthAfrica,13,0.2,1.3,0.15,9.6,0.2,4.4,0.9
Marlboro(L),AMRO,Mexico,15.8,1.8,0.89,0.13,13.9,0.3,0.8,0.3
Broadway,AMRO,Mexico,14.9,0.7,0.89,0.37,13.4,1.8,0.5,0.1
Boots,AMRO,Mexico,14.5,0.8,0.72,0.16,12.9,0.8,0.1,0.1
Derby,AMRO,Brazil,12.1,0.6,0.92,0.15,11.6,0.5,22.3,1.8
Hollywood,AMRO,Brazil,11.2,0.2,0.89,0.03,12.6,0.5,17.6,3.6
Freelowtarandnicotine,AMRO,Brazil,7.3,2.3,0.59,0.01,7.6,0.2,37.1,3.9
Marlboro(L),AMRO,Brazil,12.9,0.9,1,0.2,12.5,1.2,9.7,0.7
Doral,AMRO,USA,12.6,1,0.9,0.11,10.8,0.7,16.4,1.2
Marlboro(US),AMRO,USA,13.4,0.4,1.1,0.13,9.7,0.5,15.4,0.9
Marlboro(US),EMRO,Yemen,14.7,1.3,0.83,0.05,12.1,2.6,9,1.2
Kamaran,EMRO,Yemen,11.5,0.7,0.89,0.01,11.7,2.7,2.8,0.3
Marlboro(US),EMRO,Jordan,13.4,1,0.94,0.14,12.9,0.8,15.8,2.9
```

Figure 3-8: *Weka permits comments within a data file.*

a good place to put annotations about the source of the data and other important details. RapidMiner also has an option for annotations; you can use the graphic user interface to enter annotations for individual rows of data (see Figure 3-9).

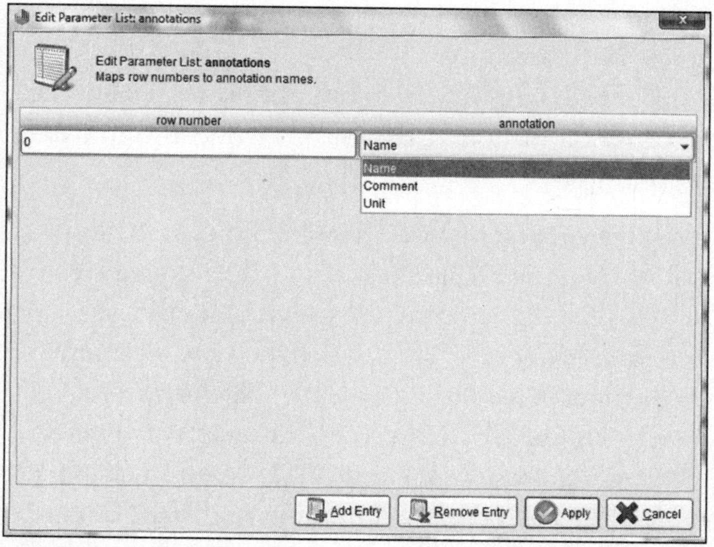

Figure 3-9: *RapidMiner offers a place to enter data annotations.*

Control case order

Data analysts often sort cases (change the order of rows) to get clearer organization for viewing data or data export. Or, you may have a functional reason to sort. For example, some applications require sorting data before merging (joining columns from different data sources).

The steps for sorting vary from one application to another. These are common options that you may find in your data analysis application:

- **Interactive sorting in a data viewer:** Look at the first variable in Figure 3-10, *Clump.* The values change from case to case, with no particular order. One click on the column header (where you see the variable name) sorts the data in ascending order of that variable, as shown in Figure 3-11. A second click re-sorts the cases in descending order (see Figure 3-12). You can click the Restore Order of Examples button to return the data to its original order.
- **Specialized sorting tools:** Data analysis applications often have sorting tools. Look for them in menus for

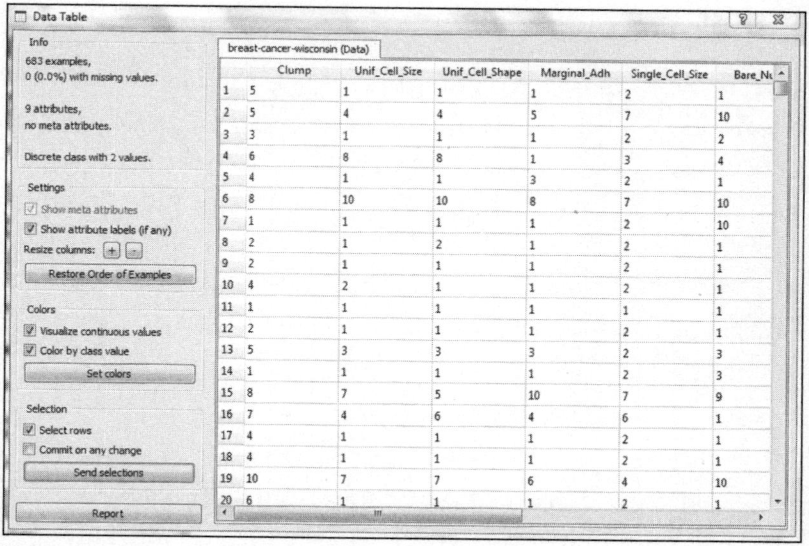

Figure 3-10: *Unsorted data.*

data manipulation. In applications with many tools, you may need to search for the right tool; just search for *sort*. Figure 3-13 shows an example; this icon represents the search function in a process. These tools can often handle complex nested sort schemes involving several variables (see Figure 3-14).

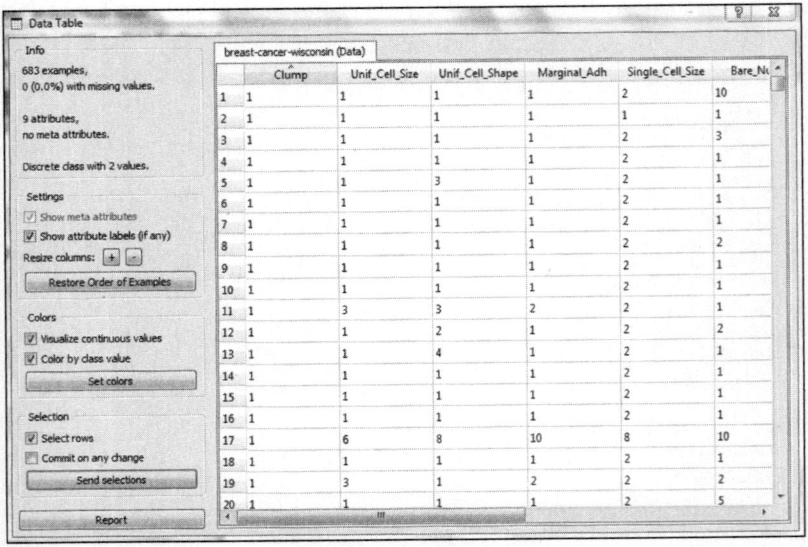

Figure 3-11: *Clicking on a column header sorts the cases.*

Get rows and columns right

A dataset with a row for each variable and a column for each case isn't organized correctly for data analysis. If your data source is structured that way, what can you do? You need something to switch the rows into columns and the columns into rows. The function that does that is called *transpose* or *flip*. (In Excel, for example, you can open the Paste menu and select Transpose.)

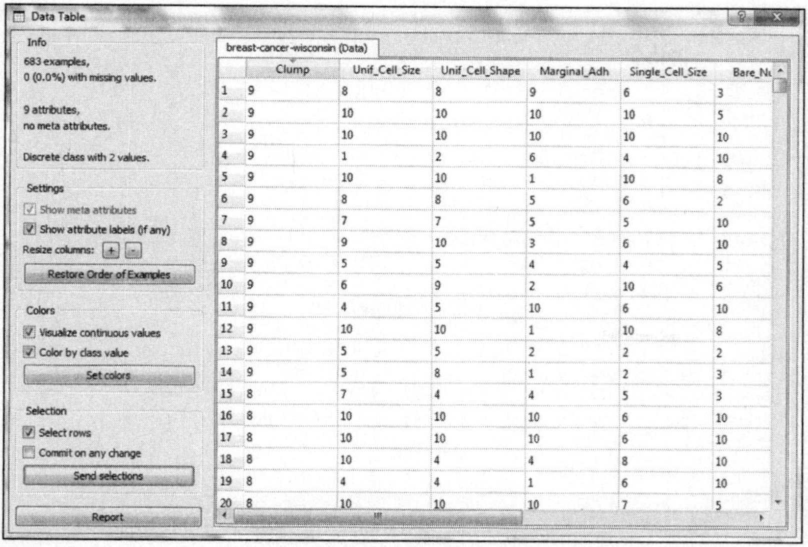

Figure 3-12: *A second click sorts in descending order.*

Put data where you need it

After you get the data and make changes to suit your needs, you have to put it somewhere. You've already saved data using spreadsheets and other applications, so you might think that knowledge will carry over to data analysis. Not completely.

In most applications, you can save data by finding that option on a menu, like the one shown in Figure 3-15, and using a file browser dialog box to indicate where you want to put a

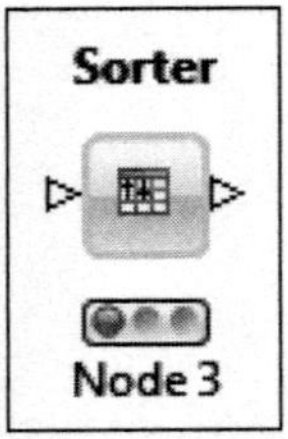

Figure 3-13: *A tool for sorting data.*

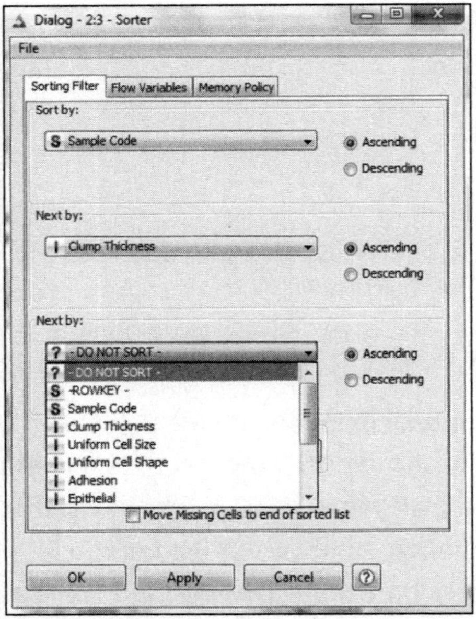

Figure 3-14: *This dialog box enables complex nested sorting.*

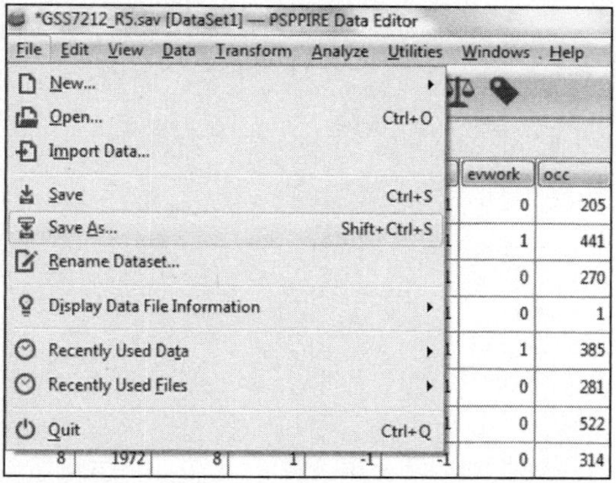

Figure 3-15: *Save As option in an application menu.*

file. But data analysis applications with visual programming interfaces are not organized that way. In your data analysis applications, you will need to find the right tool to save your data. Most data analysis applications have several tools for saving data, and their names vary from product to product, so you may have to hunt a little to find just the tool that you need.

Here's where to look for data export in several data analysis applications. These examples provide clues for finding the data export functions in any data analysis application:

- **KNIME:** Data export tools are found in the Node Repository under IO . . . Write (see Figure 3-16).

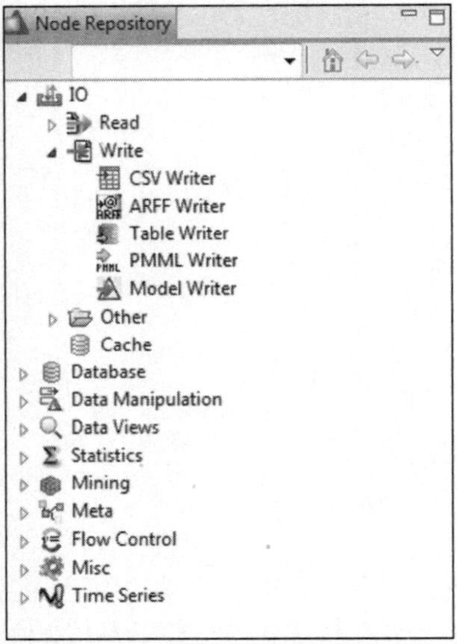

Figure 3-16: *Finding data export tools in KNIME.*

They are grouped with export tools for models as well as data.

- **Orange:** You only have one tool for saving data in this product, and it is called Save. Find it on the Widget menu under Data in Figure 3-17. In the Save dialog box (see Figure 3-18), clicking the Browse button (the one

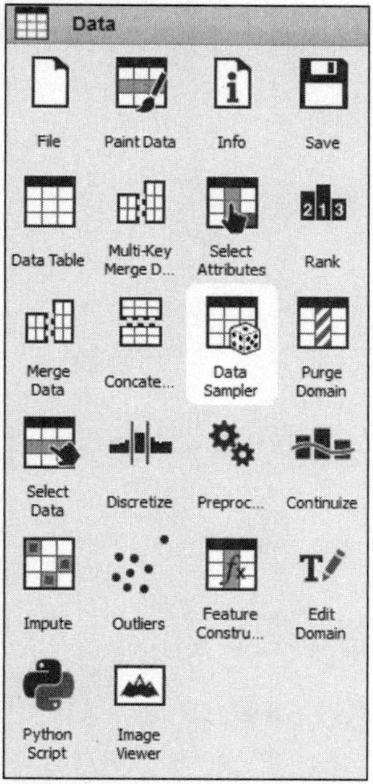

Figure 3-17: *Finding data export tools in Orange.*

with a picture of an open folder) brings up a conventional file browser dialog box (see Figure 3-19). A drop-down menu reveals data export format options.

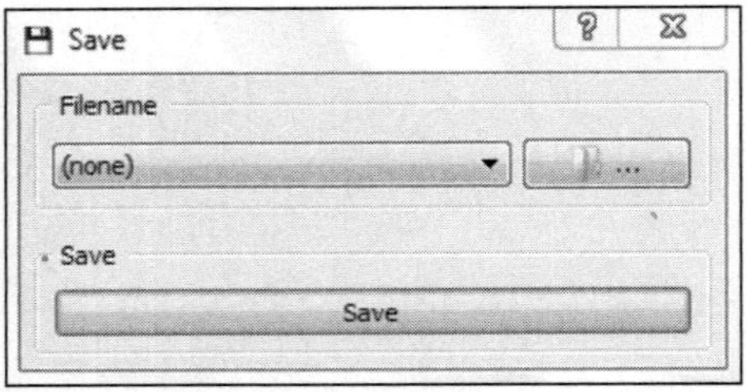

Figure 3-18: *The Save dialog box in Orange.*

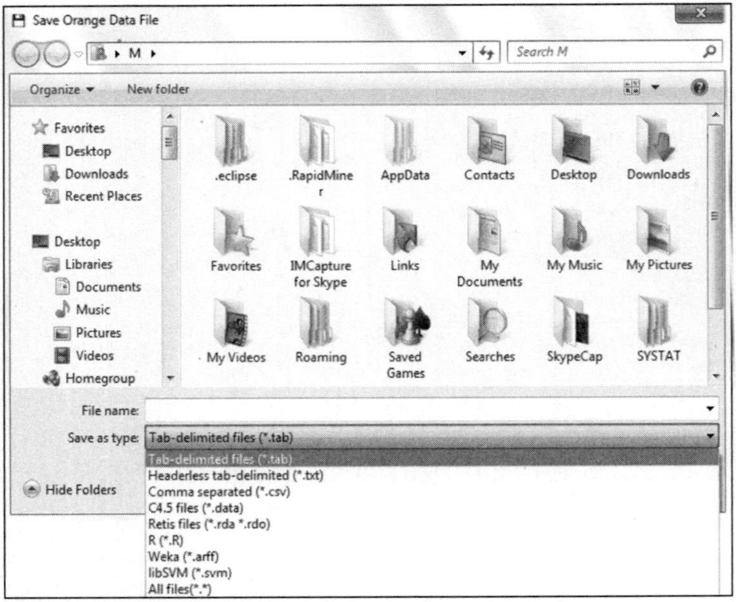

Figure 3-19: *Selecting file export type and location in Orange.*

- **RapidMiner:** Tools for data export are on the Operators menu, under Export . . . Data in Figure 3-20. You'll find a separate tool for each data format option.
- **Weka:** Look for data export on the Design menu, under DataSinks (see Figure 3-21), where it wins the award for the geekiest terminology in a data analysis application.

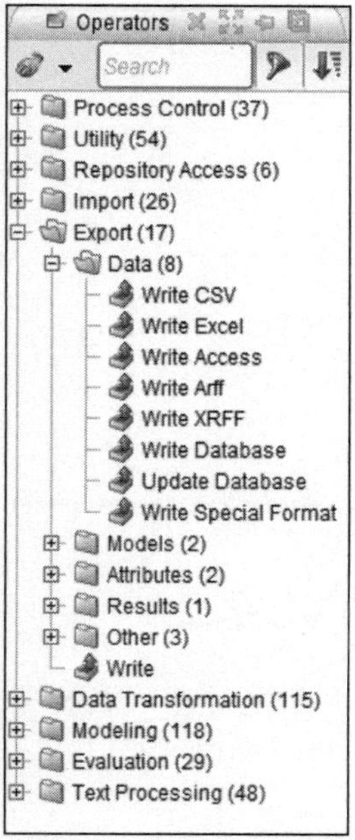

Figure 3-20: *Finding data export tools in RapidMiner.*

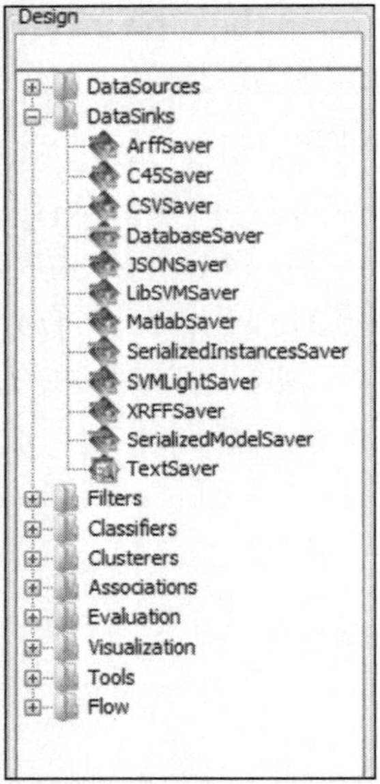

Figure 3-21: *Finding data export tools in Weka.*

Sift Out the Data You Need

Sometimes you'll have more data than you need for a given project. Here's how to pare down to just what you need.

Narrow the fields

When you have many variables in a dataset, it can be hard to find or see the ones that interest you. And if your datasets are large and you don't need all the variables, keeping the extras soaks up resources unnecessarily. So, you may need to keep some variables and drop others. Figure 3-22 shows an example in KNIME, where the right tool is called Column Filter. An example setup for this tool is shown in Figure 3-23.

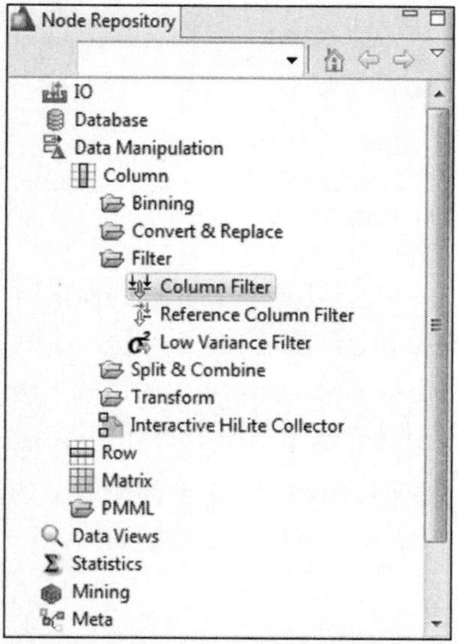

Figure 3-22: *Finding the tool to select variables in KNIME.*

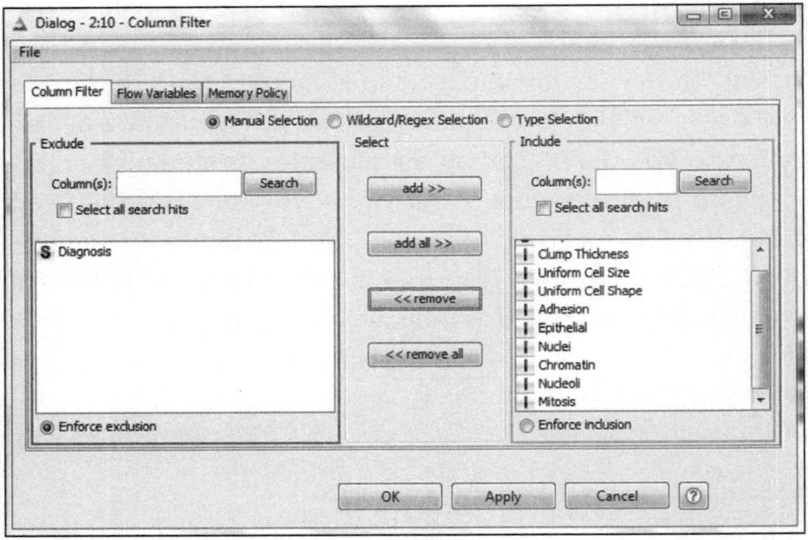

Figure 3-23: *Variable selection dialog box in KNIME.*

To narrow the fields, look for a variable selection tool in your data analysis application; these are found with other tools for data manipulation. As with other data analysis tools, the names vary from product to product. Look for variations on the words *column, variable,* or *field,* and *selection* or *filtering.*

Select relevant cases

Removing incomplete cases is one common example of data selection, or *filtering*. To select only the relevant cases for each segment that interest you, you use a data selection tool.

Figure 3-24 shows a data selection tool in a data analysis application, and Figure 3-25 shows how you'd set up that tool for a selection based on the value of a variable. It's common to use this kind of data selection, and some applications provide all sorts of built-in functions to help you define exactly the cases you want. This one has some exceptional features; it displays summary statistics for the variable and tells you exactly how many cases meet the selection criteria.

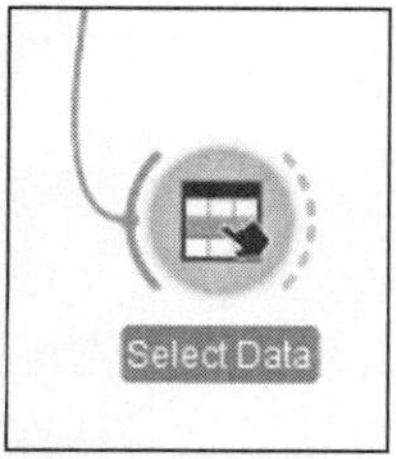

Figure 3-24: *Tool for selecting cases in Orange.*

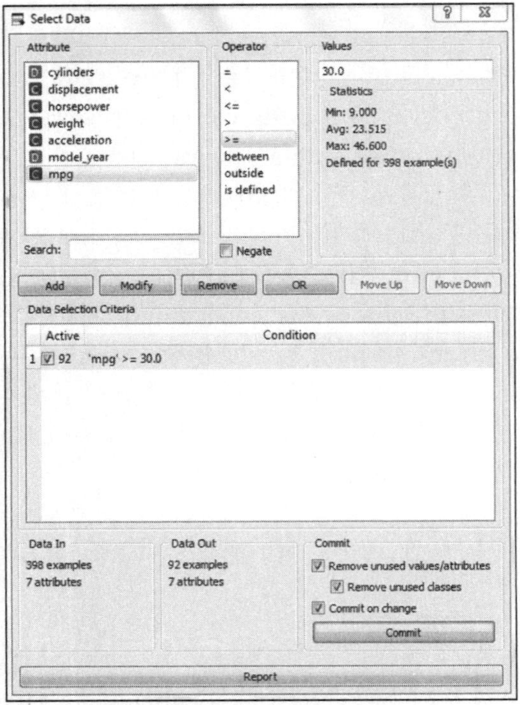

Figure 3-25: *Setting up case selection.*

Most data analysis applications have tools for selecting just the cases you need. Look in the menus (or search) for *select* or *filter.*

Use sampling tools

A popular notion these days is the more data, the better. This is not a new idea. Data analysis applications have always been developed to work with large quantities of data. But often, working with a sample of your data will give you information that is just as useful, make your work easier, and conserve your time and resources.

Sampling plays an important role in data analysis. First, the data is balanced. That means that the model uses equal numbers of cases in each of the groups being compared, even if one group has many more cases than the other in the original data. Later, the data could be split: separated into one subset to use for training a model and another for testing, for example. Using only a sample of data can also make it easier to view and interpret. Perhaps most important of all, sampling reduces the amount of data, so things run faster.

It's not always obvious where to find sampling tools in data analysis applications. Look for names that are variations on the word *sample* or *split*. Figure 3-26 shows one example, buried three layers into a menu in KNIME. Finding it may be the hardest part. The tool itself appears in Figure 3-27. Setup

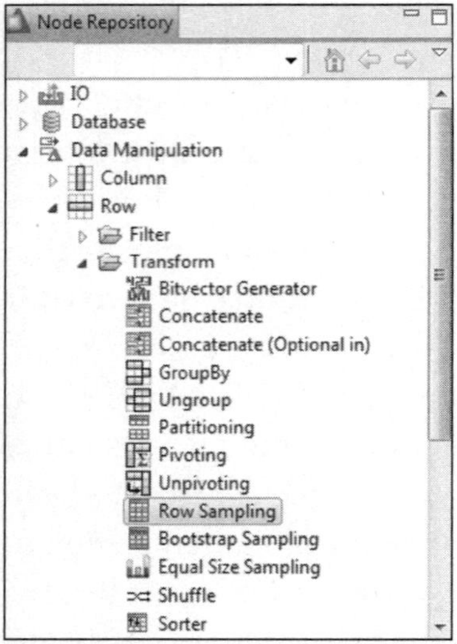

Figure 3-26: *Finding the sampling tool in KNIME.*

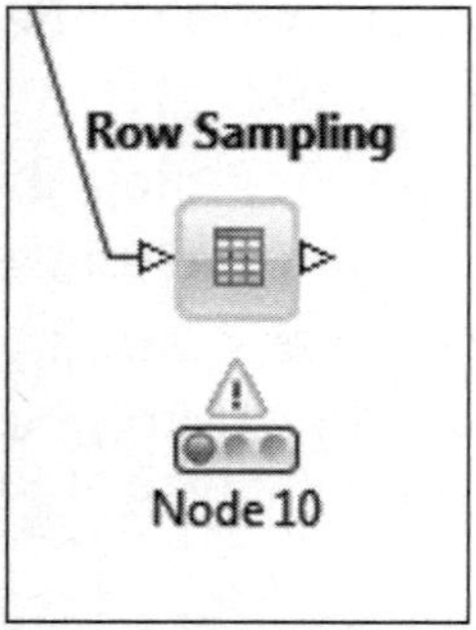

Figure 3-27: *Row Sampling tool in KNIME.*

(see Figure 3-28) may vary from application to application, but all of them give you some way to take simple random samples from your data.

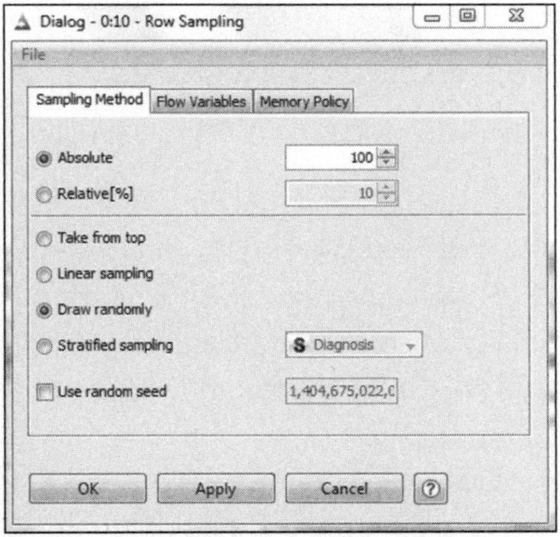

Figure 3-28: *Sampling dialog box in KNIME.*

Get the Data Together

When your data is in more than one place, you need ways to put it all together.

Merging

When you join two datasets with different variables, you're *merging* data. Merging is a common operation that's used frequently in data analysis, combining linked data such as

- Customer records and marketing campaign data
- Before-and-after test results
- Internal and vendor data

To merge datasets, you must have a variable that identifies cases for matching; this is called a *key* or *identifier* variable. And you may have to identify one of the datasets as *primary;* the primary table must have only one case for any value of the key variable.

Some data analysis applications have more than one tool for merging datasets. Figure 3-29 shows the tool for basic merges, and Figure 3-30 shows the tool for setting up more complex merge criteria.

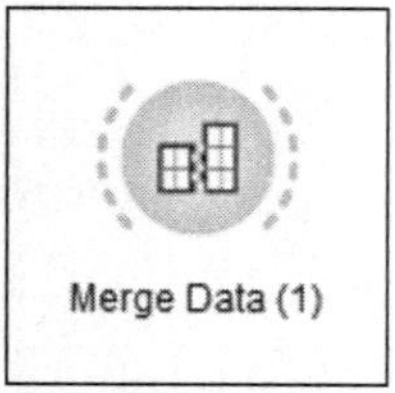

Figure 3-29: *Merge Data tool in Orange.*

Figure 3-30: *Multi-Key Merge Data tool in Orange.*

Appending

If your data sources contain the same variables (more or less; the match does not have to be identical) but different cases, joining them is called *appending* or concatenation. Like merging, this is a common operation. It's used whenever you have new cases for something that you've already been tracking. (Figure 3-31 shows a tool for appending.) The tricky part of finding the right tool is often figuring out what it's called. Look in the menus (or search) for *append, concatenate,* or *merge rows.*

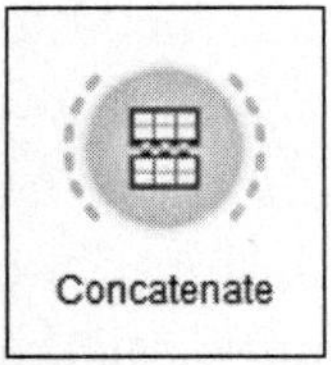

Figure 3-31: *The Concatenate tool in Orange is used for appending rows to a dataset.*

Make New Data from Old Data

The following sections deal with using your business knowledge to create relevant new data constructs from existing data.

Derive new variables

Need to add Variable A plus Variable B to make Variable C? You're *deriving* a new variable.

The calculations that you require to make your new variable might be a lot more complex than just adding two columns together. If so, you can use special functions to help with the process: Standard mathematical functions, statistical functions, string manipulation, and others are all available to you.

TIP

When you have a continuous variable and need to group the values (such as grouping test scores into percentile ranges or model scores into deciles), the function you need is *binning*. You may find it in the same tool as other similar functions or in a special tool designed especially for this purpose.

Aggregation

Summarizing data, finding totals, and calculating averages and other descriptive measures are probably not new to you. When you need your summaries in the form of new data, rather than reports, the process is called *aggregation*. Aggregated data can become the basis for additional calculations, merged with other datasets, used in any way that other data is used.

Sooner or later, you'll need to aggregate a whole dataset. But when you want to total or average all the data in a dataset, you may run into a problem: What's your grouping variable? The trick is to use a variable with a constant value for the whole dataset. So, create a variable where every value is the same, and then use it as your grouping variable.

Time-Saving Tools

Data preparation takes a lot of time. Your data analysis application may have distinctive time-saving tools already built in and waiting for you, but you won't know it if you don't make a point to see what's there. Make the data analysis process easier and faster by looking for and using special tools for purposes like these:

- **Addressing missing values:** When your data isn't complete, you may need to remove incomplete cases or make intelligent substitutions for blanks. (If the right tool isn't called something obvious, like *missing values,* look for *imputation.*)
- **Weighting:** Need some cases (or fields) to count more than others? Look for *weighting*.
- **Split file:** Need to do the same actions for each value of a variable? Look for *split file* or *looping* functions.

4

Explore Big-Data Sources and Tools

There's a lot of hype around big data these days, but most people don't really know or understand what it is or how they can use it to improve their lives and livelihoods. This chapter defines the term "big data," explains where big data comes from and how it's used, and outlines the roles that data engineers and data analysts play in the big-data ecosystem. In this chapter, you learn the fundamental big-data concepts that you need to start generating your own ideas and plans on how to leverage big data and data analysis to improve your business workflow.

Define Big Data by the Three Vs

Big data is data that exceeds the processing capacity of conventional database systems because it's too big, it moves too fast, or it doesn't fit the structural requirements of traditional database architectures. Whether data volumes rank in the terabyte or petabyte scales, data-engineered solutions must be designed to meet requirements for the data's intended destination and use.

Three characteristics — known as "the three Vs" — define big data: volume, velocity, and variety. Because the three Vs of big data are continually expanding, newer, more innovative data technologies must continuously be developed to manage big-data problems.

Volume

The lower limit of big-data *volume* starts as low as 1 terabyte, and it has no upper limit. If your organization owns at least 1 terabyte of data, it's probably a good candidate for a big-data deployment.

Be aware that in its raw form, most big data is *low value* — in other words, the value-to-data-quantity ratio is low in raw big data. Big data is composed of huge numbers of very small transactions that come in a variety of formats. These incremental components of big data produce true value only after they're aggregated and analyzed. Data engineers have the job of gathering big data, and data analysts have the job of analyzing big data.

Velocity

In engineering terms, data *velocity* is data volume per unit time. These days a lot of big data is created through automated processes and instrumentation, and because data storage costs are relatively inexpensive, system velocity is, many times, the limiting factor. Remember, big data is low value. Consequently, you need systems that can ingest a lot of data, in short order, to generate timely and valuable insights.

Big data enters an average system at velocities ranging between 30 kilobytes (K) per second to as much as 30 gigabytes (GB) per second. Many data-engineered systems are required to have a latency of less than 100 milliseconds, measured from the time the data is created to the time the system responds.

Throughput requirements can easily be as high as 1,000 messages per second in big-data systems. High-velocity, real-time moving data presents an obstacle to timely decision making. The capabilities of data-handling and data-processing technologies often limit data velocities.

Variety

Big data gets even more complicated when you add unstructured and semi-structured data to structured data sources. This *high-variety* data comes from a multitude of sources. Most importantly, it's composed of a combination of datasets with different underlying structures (structured, unstructured, or semi-structured):

- *Structured* data can be stored, processed, and manipulated in a traditional relational database management system (RDBMS). This data can be generated by humans or machines, and is derived from all sorts of sources, from clickstreams and web-based forms to point-of-sale transactions and sensors.
- *Unstructured* data comes completely disorganized — it's commonly generated from human activities and doesn't

fit into a structured database format. Such data could be derived from blog posts, emails, and Word documents.

- *Semi-structured* data doesn't fit into a structured database system, but is nonetheless structured by tags that are useful for creating a form of order and hierarchy in the data. Semi-structured data is commonly found in databases and file systems. It can be stored as log files, XML files, or JSON data files.

Heterogeneous, high-variety data is often composed of any combination of graph data, JSON files, XML files, social media data, structured tabular data, web log data, and data that's generated from clickstreams (the virtual paths that people take while surfing the web).

Identify Big-Data Sources

Big data is being continually generated by humans, machines, and sensors everywhere. Typical sources include data from social media, financial transactions, health records, clickstreams, log files, and the *Internet of things* — a web of digital connections that joins together the ever-expanding array of electronic devices we use in our everyday lives. Figure 4-1 shows a variety of popular big-data sources.

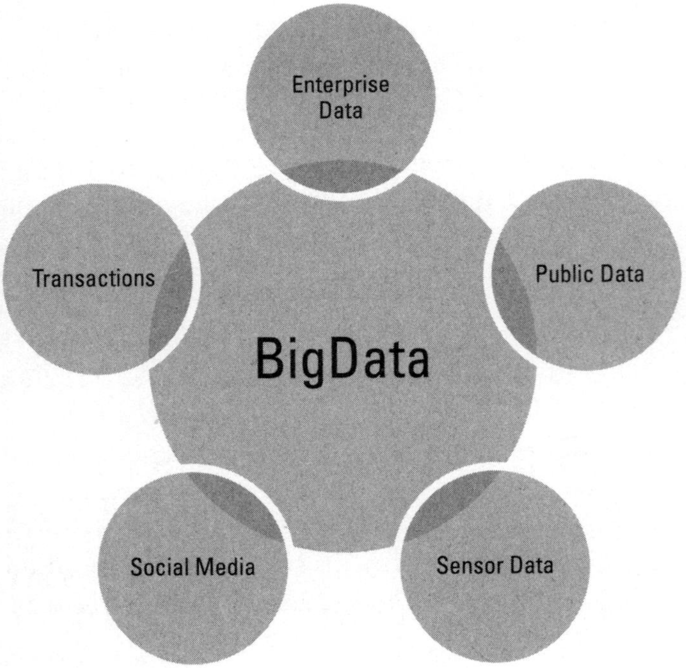

Figure 4-1: *Popular sources of big data.*

Data Analysis versus Data Engineering

Data analysis and data engineering are two different branches within the *big-data paradigm* — an approach in which huge velocities, varieties, and volumes of structured, unstructured, and semi-structured data are captured, processed, stored, and analyzed using a set of techniques and technologies that is completely novel compared to those that were used in decades past.

Both data analysis and data engineering are useful for deriving knowledge and actionable insights from raw data. Both are essential elements for any comprehensive decision-support system, and both are extremely helpful when formulating robust strategies for future business management and growth. Although the terms *data analysis* and *data engineering* are often used interchangeably, they're distinct domains of expertise. In the following sections, I introduce concepts that are fundamental to data analysis and data engineering, and then I show you the differences in how these two roles function in an organization's data-processing system.

Define data analysis

Data analysis is the use of mathematical techniques and algorithmic approaches to derive solutions to complex business and scientific problems. Data analysis practitioners use its predictive methods to derive insights that are otherwise unattainable. In business and in science, data analysis methods can provide more robust decision-making capabilities:

- **In business,** the purpose of data analysis is to empower businesses and organizations with the data information that they need to optimize organizational processes for maximum efficiency and revenue generation.
- **In science,** data analysis methods are used to derive results and develop protocols for achieving the specific scientific goal at hand.

Data analysis is a vast and multidisciplinary field. To call yourself a true data analyst, you need to have expertise in math and statistics, computer programming, and your own domain-specific subject matter.

Using data analysis skills, you can do things like:

- Use machine learning to optimize energy usages and lower corporate carbon footprints.

- Optimize tactical strategies to achieve goals in business and science.
- Predict contaminant levels from sparse environmental datasets.
- Design automated theft- and fraud-prevention systems to detect anomalies and trigger alarms based on algorithmic results.
- Craft site-recommendation engines for use in land acquisitions and real estate development.
- Implement and interpret predictive analytics and forecasting techniques for net increases in business value.

Data analysts must have extensive and diverse quantitative expertise to be able to solve these types of problems.

Define data engineering

Data engineering is the use of computer science tools and software engineering to design systems for, and solve problems with, handling and manipulating big datasets. Data engineers often have experience working with and designing real-time processing frameworks and massively parallel processing platforms (discussed later in this chapter), as well as RDBMSs.

They generally code in Java, C++, Scala, and Python. They know how to deploy Hadoop MapReduce or Spark (also discussed later in this chapter) to handle, process, and refine big data into more manageably sized datasets. Simply put, with respect to data analysis, the purpose of data engineering is to engineer big-data solutions by building coherent, modular, and scalable data-processing platforms from which data analysts can subsequently derive insights.

Using data engineering skills, you can, for example:

- Build large-scale Software-as-a-Service (SaaS) applications.
- Build and customize Hadoop and MapReduce applications.
- Design and build relational databases and highly scaled distributed architectures for processing big data.
- Build an integrated platform that simultaneously solves problems in data ingestion, data storage, machine learning, and system management — all from one interface. (*Machine learning* is the practice of applying algorithms to learn from, and make automated predictions about, data.)

Data engineers need solid skills in computer science, database design, and software engineering to be able to perform this type of work.

Compare data analysts and data engineers

The roles of data analyst and data engineer are frequently completely confused and intertwined by hiring managers. If you look at most job descriptions for companies that are hiring, they often mismatch the titles and roles or simply expect applicants to do both data analysis and data engineering.

Because many organizations combine and confuse roles in their data projects, data analysts are sometime stuck spending a lot of time learning to do the job of a data engineer, and vice versa. To get the highest-quality work product in the least amount of time, hire a data engineer to process your data and a data analyst to make sense of it for you.

Keep in mind that data engineer and data analyst are just two small roles within a larger organizational structure. Managers, middle-level employees, and organizational leaders also play a huge part in the success of any data-driven initiative. The primary benefit of incorporating data analysis and data engineering into your projects is to leverage your external and internal data to strengthen your organization's decision-support capabilities.

Make Sense of Data in Hadoop

Because big data's three Vs (volume, velocity, and variety) don't allow for the handling of big data using traditional relational database management systems, data engineers had to become innovative. To get around the limitations of relational systems, data engineers turn to the Hadoop data-processing platform to boil down big data into smaller datasets that are more manageable for data analysts to analyze.

When you hear people use the term *Hadoop* nowadays, they're generally referring to a Hadoop ecosystem that includes the Hadoop distributed file system for data storage, MapReduce for bulk data processing, Spark for real-time data processing, and YARN (Yet Another Resource Negotiator) for resource management.

In the following sections, I introduce you to MapReduce, Spark, and the Hadoop distributed file system. I also introduce the programming languages you can use to develop applications in these frameworks.

MapReduce

MapReduce is a parallel distributed processing framework that can be used to process tremendous volumes of data *in-batch* — where data is collected and then processed as one unit with processing completion times in a matter of hours or days. MapReduce works by converting raw data to sets of tuples and then combining and reducing those tuples into smaller sets of tuples. (With respect to MapReduce, *tuples* refer to key-value pairs by which data is grouped, sorted, and processed.) In layman's terms, MapReduce uses parallel distributed computing to transform big data into manageable-size data.

MapReduce jobs implement a sequence of map tasks and reduce tasks across a distributed set of servers. In the *map task,* you delegate data to key-value pairs, transform it, and filter it. Then you assign the data to nodes for processing. In the *reduce task,* you aggregate that data down to smaller-size datasets. Data from the reduce step is transformed into a standard *key-value format* — where the *key* acts as the record identifier and the *value* is the value being identified by the key. The clusters' computing nodes process the map tasks and reduce tasks that are defined by the user.

This work is done in two steps:

1. **Map the data.** The incoming data must first be delegated into key-value pairs and divided into fragments, which are then assigned to map tasks. Each *computing cluster* (a group of nodes that are connected to each other and perform a shared computing task) is assigned a number of map tasks, which are subsequently distributed among its nodes. Upon processing of the key-value pairs, intermediate key-value pairs are generated. The intermediate key-value pairs are sorted by their key values, and this list is divided into a new set of fragments. Whatever count you have for these new fragments, it will be the same as the count for the reduce tasks.
2. **Reduce the data.** Every reduce task has a fragment assigned to it. The reduce task processes the fragment and produces an output, which is also a key-value pair. Reduce tasks are also distributed among the different nodes of the cluster. After the task is completed, the final output is written onto a file system.

In short, you can use MapReduce as a batch-processing tool, to boil down and make sense of a huge volume, velocity, and variety of data by using map and reduce tasks to tag the data by (key, value) pairs, and then reduce those pairs into smaller sets of data through *aggregation operations* — operations that combine multiple values from a dataset into a single value. A diagram of the MapReduce architecture is shown in Figure 4-2.

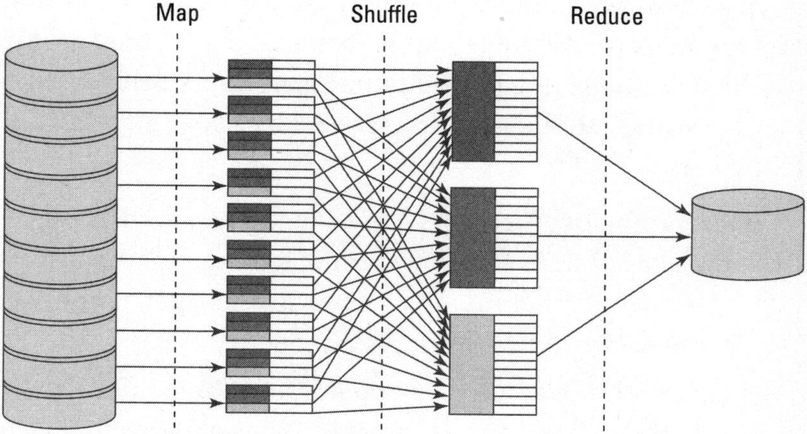

Figure 4-2: *The MapReduce architecture.*

If your data doesn't lend itself to being tagged and processed via keys, values, and aggregation, map-and-reduce generally isn't a good fit for your needs.

Real-time processing

If you need to query big-data streams in real-time, you can't do that sort of thing using MapReduce. In these cases, use a real-time processing framework instead.

A *real-time processing framework* is — as its name implies — a framework that processes data in real-time (or near-real-time) as that data streams and flows into the system. Real-time frameworks process data in micro-batches; that is, they return results in a matter of seconds rather than hours or days, like MapReduce. Real-time processing frameworks do either of the following:

- **Lower the overhead of MapReduce tasks to increase the overall time efficiency of the system:** Solutions in this category include Apache Storm and Apache Spark for near-real-time stream processing.
- **Deploy innovative querying methods to facilitate the real-time querying of big data:** Some solutions in this category are Google's Dremel, Apache Drill, Shark for Apache Hive, and Cloudera's Impala.

Although MapReduce was historically the main processing framework in a Hadoop system, Spark has recently made some major advances in assuming MapReduce's position. *Spark* is an in-memory computing application that you can use to query, explore, analyze, and even run machine learning algorithms on incoming, streaming data in near-real-time. Its power lies in its processing speed — the ability to process and make predictions from streaming big-data sources in seconds flat is no laughing matter. Major vendors such as Cloudera have been pushing for the advancement of Spark so that it can be used as a complete MapReduce replacement, but it isn't there yet.

Real-time, stream-processing frameworks are quite useful in a multitude of industries — from stock and financial market analyses to e-commerce optimizations, and from real-time fraud detection to optimized order logistics. Regardless of the industry in which you work, if your business is impacted by real-time data streams that are generated by humans, machines, or sensors, a real-time processing framework would be helpful to you in optimizing and generating value for your organization.

The Hadoop distributed file system

The Hadoop distributed file system (HDFS) uses clusters of commodity hardware for storing data. Hardware in each cluster is connected, and this hardware is composed of *commodity servers* — low-cost, low-performing generic servers that offer powerful computing capabilities when run in parallel across a shared cluster. These commodity servers are also called *nodes*. Commoditized computing dramatically decreases the costs involved in storing big data.

The HDFS is characterized by three key features:

- **HDFS blocks:** In data storage, a *block* is a storage unit that contains some maximum number of records. By default, HDFS blocks can store 64MB of data.
- **Redundancy:** Datasets that are stored in HDFS are broken up and stored on blocks. These blocks are then replicated (three times, by default) and stored on several different servers in the cluster, as backup, or *redundancy*.
- **Fault tolerance:** A system is described as *fault tolerant* if it is built to continue successful operations despite the failure of one or more of its subcomponents. Because the HDFS has built-in redundancy across multiple servers in a cluster, if one server fails, the system simply retrieves the data from another server.

TIP

Don't pay storage costs on data you don't need. Storing big data is relatively inexpensive, but it's not free. In fact, storage costs range up to $20,000 per commodity server in a Hadoop cluster. For this reason, only relevant data should be stored.

The Hadoop platform

The Hadoop platform is the premier platform for large-scale data processing, storage, and management. This open-source platform is generally composed of the HDFS, MapReduce, Spark, and YARN, all working together.

Within a Hadoop platform, the workloads of applications that run on the HDFS (like MapReduce and Spark) are divided among the nodes of the cluster, and the output is stored on the HDFS. A Hadoop cluster can be composed of thousands of nodes. To keep the costs of input/output processes low, MapReduce jobs are performed as close to the data as possible — the reduce-tasks processors are positioned as closely as possible to the outgoing map task data that needs to be processed. This design facilitates the sharing of computational requirements in big-data processing.

Hadoop also supports hierarchical organization. Some of its nodes are classified as master nodes, and others are categorized as slaves. The master service, known as *JobTracker,* is designed to control several slave services. A single slave service (called a *TaskTracker*) is distributed to each node. The JobTracker controls the TaskTrackers and assigns Hadoop MapReduce tasks to them. YARN, the resource manager, acts as an integrated system that performs resource management and scheduling functions.

Alternative Big-Data Solutions

Looking past Hadoop, alternative big-data solutions are on the horizon. These solutions make it possible to work with big data in real-time or to use alternative database technologies to handle and process data. In the following sections, I introduce you to massively parallel processing platforms and the NoSQL databases that allow you to work with big data outside of the Hadoop environment.

Massively parallel processing

Massively parallel processing (MPP) platforms can be used instead of MapReduce as an approach for distributed data processing. If your goal is to deploy parallel processing on a traditional data warehouse, an MPP may be the perfect solution.

To understand how MPP compares to a standard MapReduce parallel-processing framework, consider that MPP runs parallel computing tasks on costly, custom hardware, whereas MapReduce runs them on inexpensive commodity servers. Consequently, MPP processing capabilities are cost-restrictive. MPP is quicker and easier to use, however, than standard MapReduce jobs. That's because MPP can be queried using Structured Query Language (SQL), but native MapReduce jobs are controlled by the more complicated Java programming language.

NoSQL databases

A traditional RDBMS isn't equipped to handle big-data demands. That's because it is designed to handle only relational datasets constructed of data that's stored in clean rows and columns and thus is capable of being queried via SQL. RDBMSs are not capable of handling unstructured and semi-structured data. Moreover, RDBMSs don't have the processing and handling capabilities that are needed for meeting big-data volume and velocity requirements.

This is where NoSQL comes in. *NoSQL* databases are non-relational, distributed database systems that were designed to rise to the big-data challenge. NoSQL databases step out past the traditional relational database architecture and offer a much more scalable, efficient solution. NoSQL systems facilitate non-SQL data querying of non-relational, semi-structured, and unstructured data. In this way, NoSQL databases can handle the structured, semi-structured, and unstructured data sources that are common in big-data systems.

NoSQL offers four categories of non-relational databases: graph databases, document databases, key-values stores, and column family stores. Because NoSQL offers native functionality for each of these separate types of data structures, it offers efficient storage and retrieval functionality for most types of non-relational data. This adaptability and efficiency makes NoSQL an increasingly popular choice for handling big data and for overcoming the processing challenges that come along with it.

The NoSQL applications Apache Cassandra and MongoDB are used for data storage and real-time processing. Apache Cassandra is a popular type of key-value store NoSQL database, and MongoDB is a document-oriented type of NoSQL database. It uses dynamic schemas and stores JSON-esque documents. MongoDB is the most popular type of document store on the NoSQL market.

5

Apply Data-Driven Insights to Business and Industry

To the nerds and geeks out there, data analysis is interesting in its own right, but to most people, it's interesting only because of the benefits it can generate. Most business managers and organizational leaders couldn't care less about data and complex statistical algorithms. They are, on the other hand, extremely interested in finding new ways to increase business profits by increasing sales rates and decreasing inefficiencies. In this chapter, you learn about the concept of business-centric data analysis, understand how it differs from traditional business intelligence, and see how you can use data-derived business insights to increase your business's bottom line.

The Benefits of Business-Centric Data Analysis

Business is complex. Data analysis is complex. At times, it's easy to get so caught up looking at the trees that you forget to look for a way out of the forest. That's why, in all areas of business, it's extremely important to stay focused on the end goal. Ultimately, no matter what line of business you're in, true north is always the same: business profit growth. Whether you achieve that growth by creating greater efficiencies or by increasing sales rates and customer loyalty, the end goal is to create a more stable, solid profit-growth rate for your business. The following list describes some of the ways that you can use business-centric data analysis and business intelligence to help increase profits:

- **Decrease financial risks.** A business-centric data analyst can decrease financial risk in e-commerce business by using time series anomaly-detection methods for real-time fraud detection; for example, to decrease

Card-Not-Present fraud or to decrease the incidence of account takeovers.

- **Increase the efficiencies of systems and processes.** This is a business systems optimization function that's performed by both the business-centric data analyst and the business analyst. Both use analytics to optimize business processes, structures, and systems, but their methods and data sources differ. The end goal here should be to decrease needless resource expenditures and to increase return on investment for justified expenditures.
- **Increase sales rates.** To increase sales rates for your offerings, you can employ a business-centric data analyst to help you find the best ways to upsell and cross-sell, increase customer loyalty, increase conversions in each layer of the funnel, and exact-target your advertising and discounts. It's likely that your business is already employing many of these tactics, but a business-centric data analyst can look at all data related to the business and, from that, derive insights that supercharge these efforts.

Convert Raw Data into Actionable Insights with Data Analytics

Turning your raw data into actionable insights is the first step in the progression from the data you've collected to something that actually benefits you. Business-centric data analysts use *data analytics* to generate insights from raw data.

Types of analytics

Listed here, in order of increasing complexity, are the four types of data analytics you'll most likely encounter:

- **Descriptive analytics:** This type of analytics answers the question, "What happened?" Descriptive analytics are based on historical and current data. A business analyst or a business-centric data analyst bases modern-day business intelligence on descriptive analytics.
- **Diagnostic analytics:** This type of analytics answers the question, "Why did this particular something happen?"

or "What went wrong?" Diagnostic analytics are useful for deducing and inferring the success or failure of subcomponents of any data-driven initiative.

- **Predictive analytics:** This type of analytics answers the question, "What will (or might) happen?" Although this type of analytics is based on historical and current data, predictive analytics go one step further than descriptive analytics. Predictive analytics involve complex model-building and analysis in order to predict a future event or trend. In a business context, these analyses would be performed by the business-centric data analyst.
- **Prescriptive analytics:** This type of analytics answers the question, "What should we do to make a predicted future event or trend happen?" This type of analytics aims to optimize processes, structures, and systems through informed action that's based on predictive analytics — essentially telling you what you should do based on an informed estimation of what will happen. Both business analysts and business-centric data analysts can generate prescriptive analytics, but their methods and data sources differ.

Ideally, a business should engage in all four types of data analytics, but prescriptive analytics is the most direct and effective means by which to generate value from data insights.

Common challenges in analytics

Analytics commonly pose at least two challenges in the business enterprise. First, organizations often have difficulty finding new hires with specific skill sets that include analytics. Second, even skilled analysts often have difficulty communicating complex insights in a way that's understandable to management decision-makers.

To overcome these challenges, the organization must create and nurture a culture that values and accepts analytics products. The business must work to educate all levels of the organization so that management has a basic concept of analytics and the success that can be achieved by implementing them. Conversely, business-centric data analysts must have a solid working knowledge about business in general and, in particular, a solid understanding of the business at hand. A strong business knowledge is one of the three main requirements of any business-centric data analyst; the other two are a strong coding acumen and strong quantitative analysis skills via math and statistical modeling.

Data wrangling

Data wrangling is another important portion of the work that's required in order to convert data to insights. To build analytics from raw data, you'll almost always need to use *data wrangling* — the processes and procedures that you use to clean and convert data from one format and structure to another so that the data is accurate and in the format that analytics tools and scripts require for consumption. The following sections highlight some of the practices and issues that are most relevant to data wrangling.

Data extraction

The business-centric data analyst must first identify which datasets are relevant to the problem at hand and then extract sufficient quantities of the data that's required to solve the problem. (This extraction process is commonly referred to as *data mining*.)

Data preparation

Data preparation involves cleaning the raw data extracted through data mining and then converting it into a format that allows for a more convenient consumption of the data. Six steps are involved in data preparation:

1. **Import.** Read relevant datasets into your application.
2. **Clean.** Remove strays, duplicates, and out-of-range records, and standardize casing.
3. **Transform.** Handle missing values, deal with outliers, and scale your variables.
4. **Process.** Use data parsing, recoding of variables, concatenation, and other methods of reformatting your dataset to prepare it for analysis.
5. **Log.** Create a log that describes your dataset, including descriptive statistics, information on variable formats, data source, and collection methods. Once you generate this log, make sure to store it in a place you'll remember, in case you need to share these details with other users of the processed dataset.
6. **Back up.** Store a backup of this processed dataset so that you have a clean, fresh version — no matter what.

Data governance

Data governance standards are used as a quality control measure to ensure that manual and automated data sources conform to the data standards of the model at hand. Data governance standards must be applied so that the data is at the right granularity when it's stored and made ready for use. (*Granularity* is a measure of a dataset's level of detail. Data granularity is determined by the relative size of the subgroupings into which the data is divided.)

Data architecture

IT architecture is key. If your data is isolated in separate, fixed repositories — those infamous *data silos* everybody complains about — then it's available to only a few people within a particular line of business. Siloed data structures result in scenarios where a majority of an organization's data is simply unavailable for use by the organization at large. This makes siloed data structures incredibly wasteful and inefficient.

Take action on business insights

After wrangling your data down to actionable insights, the second step in the progression from raw data to value-added is to take decisive actions based on those insights. In business, the only justifiable purpose for spending time deriving insights from raw data is that the actions should lead to an increase in business profits. Failure to take action on data-driven insights results in a complete and total loss of the resources that were spent deriving them, at no benefit whatsoever to the organization. An organization absolutely must be ready and equipped to change, evolve, and progress when new business insights become available.

To best prepare your organization to take action on insights derived from business data, make sure you have the following people and systems in place:

- **Right data, right time, right place:** Have the right data, collected and made available at the right time and place, when it's needed the most.
- **Business-centric data analysts and business analysts:** Have business-centric data analysts and business analysts in place and ready to tackle problems when they arise.
- **Educated and enthusiastic management:** Educate and encourage your organization's leaders so that you have a management team that understands, values, and

makes effective use of business insights gleaned from analytics.

- **Informed and enthusiastic organizational culture:** If the culture of your organization reflects a naïveté or lack of understanding about the value of data, begin fostering a corporate culture that values data insights and analytics. Consider using training, workshops, and events.
- **Written procedures with clearly designated chains of responsibility:** Have documented processes in place and interwoven into your organization so that when the time comes, the organization is prepared to respond. New insights are generated all the time, but growth is achieved only through iterative adjustments and actions based on constantly evolving data insights. The organization needs to have clearly defined procedures ready to accommodate these changes as necessary.
- **Advancement in technology:** Your enterprise must keep up to date with rapidly changing technological developments in the analytics space. There are many ways to keep up. If you employ in-house experts, you can assign them the ongoing responsibility of monitoring industry advancements and then

suggesting changes that are needed to keep your organization current. You can also purchase cloud-based Software-as-a-Service (SaaS) subscriptions and then rely on SaaS platform upgrades to keep you up to speed on the most innovative and cutting-edge technologies.

Distinguish between Business Intelligence and Data Analysis

Business-centric data analysts and business analysts who do business intelligence are like cousins: They both use data to work toward the same business goal, but their approach, technology, and function differ by measurable degrees. In the following sections I define, compare, and distinguish between business intelligence and business-centric data analysis.

Business intelligence, defined

The purpose of business intelligence (BI) is to convert raw data into business insights that business leaders and managers can use to make data-informed decisions. Business analysts use business intelligence tools to create products that help business managers make decisions. If you want to build decision-support dashboards, visualizations, or reports from complete medium-size sets of structured business data, you can use business intelligence tools and methods to help you.

Business intelligence (BI) is composed of

- **Mostly internal datasets:** Business data and information that's supplied by your organization's managers and stakeholders.
- **Tools, technologies, and skill sets:** Examples here include online analytical processing, ETL (extracting, transforming, and loading data from one database into another), data warehousing, and information technology for business applications. These are discussed in more detail in "Useful technologies and skill sets in business intelligence," later in this chapter.

The kinds of data used in business intelligence

Insights that are generated in business intelligence are derived from standard-size sets of structured business data. BI solutions are mostly built from *transactional data* — data that's generated during the course of a transaction event, such as data generated during a sale or during a money transfer between bank accounts. Transactional data is a natural byproduct of business activities that occur across an organization, and all sorts of inferences can be derived from it. The following list describes the possible questions you can answer by using BI to derive insights from these types of data:

- **Customer service:** "What areas of business are causing the largest customer wait times?"
- **Sales and marketing:** "Which marketing tactics are most effective and why?"
- **Operations:** "How efficiently is the help desk operating? Are there any immediate actions that must be taken to remedy a problem there?"
- **Employee performance:** "Which employees are the most productive? Which are the least productive?"

Useful technologies and skill sets in business intelligence

To streamline BI functions, make sure that your data is organized for optimal ease of access and presentation. You can use multidimensional databases to help you. Unlike relational or *flat* databases, *multidimensional* databases organize data into cubes that are stored as multidimensional arrays. If you want your BI staff to be able to work with source data as quickly and easily as possible, you can use multidimensional databases to store data in a cube rather than store the data across several relational databases that may or may not be compatible with one another.

This cubic data structure enables *Online Analytical Processing (OLAP)* — a technology that allows you to quickly and easily access and use your data for all sorts of different operations and analyses. To illustrate the concept of OLAP, imagine that you have a cube of sales data that has three dimensions: time, region, and business unit. You can *slice* the data to view only one rectangle — one sales region, for example. You can *dice* the data to view a smaller cube made up of some subset of time, region(s), and business unit(s). You can *drill down* or *drill up* to view either highly detailed or highly summarized data, respectively. And you can *roll up,* or total, the numbers along one dimension — to total business unit numbers, for example, or to view sales across time and region only.

OLAP is just one type of *data warehousing system* — a centralized data repository that you can use to store and access your data. A more traditional data warehouse system commonly employed in business intelligence solutions is a *data mart* — a data storage system that you can use to store one particular area of data, belonging to only one line of business in the enterprise. Extract, transform, and load (ETL) is the process that you'd use to extract data, transform it, and load it into your database or data warehouse. Business analysts generally have strong backgrounds and training in business and information technology. As a discipline, BI relies on traditional IT technologies and skills.

Business-Centric Data Analysis

Within the business enterprise, data analysis serves the same purpose that business intelligence does — to convert raw data into business insights that business leaders and managers can use to make data-informed decisions. If you have large sets of structured and unstructured data sources that may or may not be complete and you want to convert those sources into valuable insights for decision support across the enterprise, call on a data analyst. Business-centric data analysis is multidisciplinary and incorporates the following elements:

- **Quantitative analysis:** Can be in the form of mathematical modeling, *multivariate* statistical analysis (a simultaneous statistical analysis of more than one variable at a time), forecasting, and/or simulations.
- **Programming skills:** You need the necessary programming skills to analyze raw data *and* to make this data accessible to business users.
- **Business knowledge:** You need knowledge of the business and its environment so that you can better understand the relevancy of your findings.

Data analysis is a pioneering discipline. Data analysts often employ the scientific method for data exploration, hypotheses formation, and hypothesis testing (through simulation and statistical modeling). Business-centric data analysts generate valuable data insights, often by exploring patterns and anomalies in business data. Data analysis in a business context is commonly composed of

- **Internal and external datasets:** Data analysis is flexible. You can create business data mash-ups from internal and external sources of structured and unstructured data fairly easily. (A *data mash-up* is combination of two or more data sources that are then analyzed together in order to provide users with a more complete view of the situation at hand.)
- **Tools, technologies, and skill sets:** Examples here could involve using cloud-based platforms, statistical and mathematical programming, machine learning, data analysis using Python and R, and advanced data visualization.

Like business analysts, business-centric data analysts produce decision-support products for business managers and organizational leaders to use. These products include analytics dashboards and data visualizations, but generally not tabular data reports and tables.

Useful data in business-centric data analysis

You can use data analysis to derive business insights from standard-size sets of structured business data (just like BI) or from structured, semi-structured, and unstructured sets of big data. Data analysis solutions are not confined to transactional data that sits in a relational database; you can use data analysis to create valuable insights from all available data sources. These data sources include

- **Transactional business data:** This type of structured data is used in traditional BI and includes management data, customer service data, sales and marketing data, operational data, and employee performance data.
- **Social data related to the brand or business:** This type of data includes unstructured data generated through emails, instant messaging, and social networks such as Twitter, Facebook, LinkedIn, Pinterest, and Instagram.
- **Machine data from business operations:** Machines automatically generate this unstructured data; for example, SCADA data, machine data, or sensor data. (The acronym *SCADA* refers to Supervisory Control and Data Acquisition. SCADA systems are used to

control remotely operating mechanical systems and equipment. They generate data that is used to monitor the operations of machines and equipment.)

- **Audio, video, image, and PDF file data:** These well-established formats are all sources of unstructured data.

Useful technologies and skill sets in business-centric data analysis

Because the products of data analysis are often generated from big data, cloud-based data platform solutions are common in the field. Data that's used in data analysis is often derived from data-engineered big-data solutions, like Hadoop, MapReduce, Spark, and massively parallel processing (MPP) platforms (see Chapter 4). Data analysts are innovative forward-thinkers who must often think outside the box in order to solve problems. Many data analysts tend toward open-source solutions, when available. From a cost perspective, this approach benefits the organizations that employ these scientists.

Business-centric data analysts often use machine learning techniques to find patterns in (and derive predictive insights from) huge datasets that are related to a line of business or the business at large. They're skilled in math, statistics, and programming, and they often use these skills to generate predictive models. They generally know how to program in Python or R. Most of them know how to use SQL to query relevant data from structured databases. They are usually skilled at communicating data insights to end users — in business-centric data analysis, end users are business managers and organizational leaders. Data analysts must be skillful at using verbal, oral, and visual means to communicate valuable data insights.

How machine learning methods generate business value

A discussion of data analysis in business would be incomplete without a description of the popular machine learning methods being used to generate business value, as described in this list:

- **Linear regression:** You can use linear regression to make predictions for sales forecasts, pricing optimization, marketing optimization, and financial risk assessment.
- **Logistic regression:** Use logistic regression to predict customer churn, to predict response-versus-ad

spending, to predict the lifetime value of a customer, and to monitor how business decisions affect predicted churn rates.

- **Naïve Bayes:** If you want to build a spam detector, analyze customer sentiment, or automatically categorize products, customers, or competitors, you can do that using a Naïve Bayes classifier.
- **K-means clustering:** K-means clustering is useful for cost modeling and customer segmentation (for marketing optimization purposes).
- **Hierarchical clustering:** If you want to model business processes, or to segment customers based on survey responses, hierarchical clustering will probably come in handy.
- **k-nearest neighbor classification:** k-nearest neighbor is a type of instance-based learning. You can use it for text document classification, financial distress prediction modeling, and competitor analysis and classification.
- **Principal component analysis:** Principal component analysis is a dimensionality reduction method that you can use for detecting fraud, for speech recognition, and for spam detection.

6 Machine Learning

If you've been watching any news lately, there's no doubt that you've heard of something called *machine learning*. It's often referenced when reporters are covering stories on some new and amazing invention from artificial intelligence. In this chapter, you dip your toes into the area called machine learning.

What Is Machine Learning?

Machine learning is the practice of applying algorithmic models to data, in an iterative manner, so that your computer discovers hidden patterns or trends that you can use to make predictions. It's also called *algorithmic learning*. Machine learning has a vast and ever-expanding assortment of use cases, including

- Real-time Internet advertising
- Internet marketing personalization
- Internet search
- Spam filtering
- Recommendation engines
- Natural language processing and sentiment analysis
- Automatic facial recognition
- Customer churn prediction
- Credit score modeling
- Survival analysis for mechanical equipment

The machine learning process

Three main steps are involved in machine learning: setting up, learning, and application. Setting up involves acquiring data, preprocessing it, selecting the most appropriate variables for the task at hand, and breaking the data into training and test datasets. You use the *training data* to train the model, and the *test data* to test the accuracy of the model's predictions. The learning step involves model experimentation, training, building, and testing. The application step involves model deployment and prediction.

TIP

A good rule of thumb when breaking data into test and training sets is to apply random sampling to take two-thirds of the original dataset to use as data to train the model. Use the remaining one-third of the data as test data, for evaluating the model's predictions.

Machine learning terms

Before getting too deep into a discussion on machine learning methods, you need to know about the sometimes-confusing vocabulary associated with the field. Because machine learning is an offshoot of both traditional statistics and computer science, it has adopted terms from both fields and added a few of its own. Here are a few terms you need to know:

- **Instance:** The same as a *row* (in a data table), an *observation* (in statistics), and a *data point*. Machine learning practitioners might also call an instance a *case*.

- **Feature:** The same as a *column* or *field* (in a data table) and a *variable* (in statistics). In regression methods, a feature is also called an *independent variable* (IV).
- **Target variable:** The same as a *predictant* or *dependent variable* (DV) in statistics.

In machine learning, *feature selection* is a somewhat straightforward process for selecting appropriate variables; for *feature engineering*, you need substantial domain expertise and strong data science skills to manually design input variables from the underlying dataset. You use feature engineering in cases where your model needs a better representation of the problem being solved than is available in the raw dataset.

Learning Styles

There are three main styles within machine learning: supervised, unsupervised, and semi-supervised. Supervised and unsupervised methods are behind most modern machine learning applications, and semi-supervised learning is an up-and-coming star.

Supervised learning

Supervised learning algorithms require that input data has labeled features. These algorithms learn from known features of that data to produce an output model that successfully predicts labels for new incoming, unlabeled data points. You use supervised learning when you have a labeled dataset composed of historical values that are good predictors of future events. Use cases include survival analysis and fraud detection, among others. Logistic regression is a type of supervised learning algorithm, and you can read more on that topic in Chapter 7.

Unsupervised learning

Unsupervised learning algorithms accept unlabeled data and attempt to group observations into categories based on underlying similarities in input features, as shown in Figure 6-1. Principal component analysis, k-means clustering, and singular value decomposition are all examples of unsupervised machine learning algorithms. Popular use cases include recommendation engines, facial recognition systems, and customer segmentation.

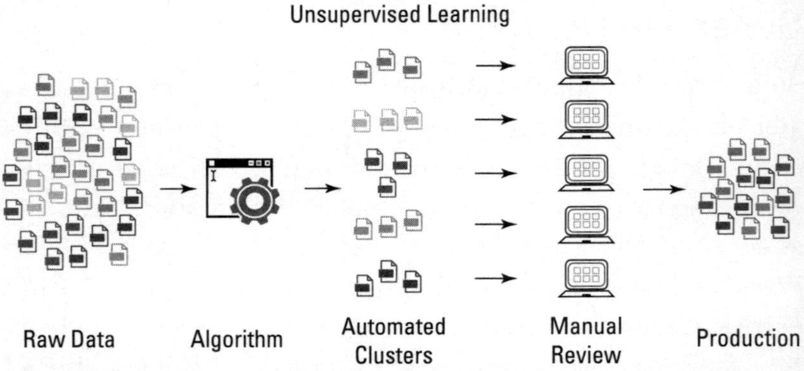

Figure 6-1: *Unsupervised machine learning breaks down unlabeled data into subgroups.*

Semi-supervised learning

Semi-supervised learning (or *reinforcement* learning) is a behavior-based learning model. It is based on a mechanism similar to how humans and animals learn. The model is given "rewards" based on how it behaves, and it subsequently learns to maximize the sum of its rewards by adapting the decisions it makes to earn as many rewards as possible. Semi-supervised learning is an up-and-coming concept in data science.

What You Can Do with Machine Learning

Whether you're just getting familiar with the algorithms that are involved in machine learning or you're looking to find out more about what's happening in cutting-edge machine learning advancements, this section has something for you. First, you see an overview of machine learning algorithms, broken down by function, and then you learn more about the advanced areas of machine learning that are embodied by deep learning and Apache Spark.

Select algorithms based on function

When you need to choose a class of machine learning algorithms, it's helpful to consider each model class based on its functionality. For the most part, algorithmic functionality falls into the categories shown in Figure 6-2.

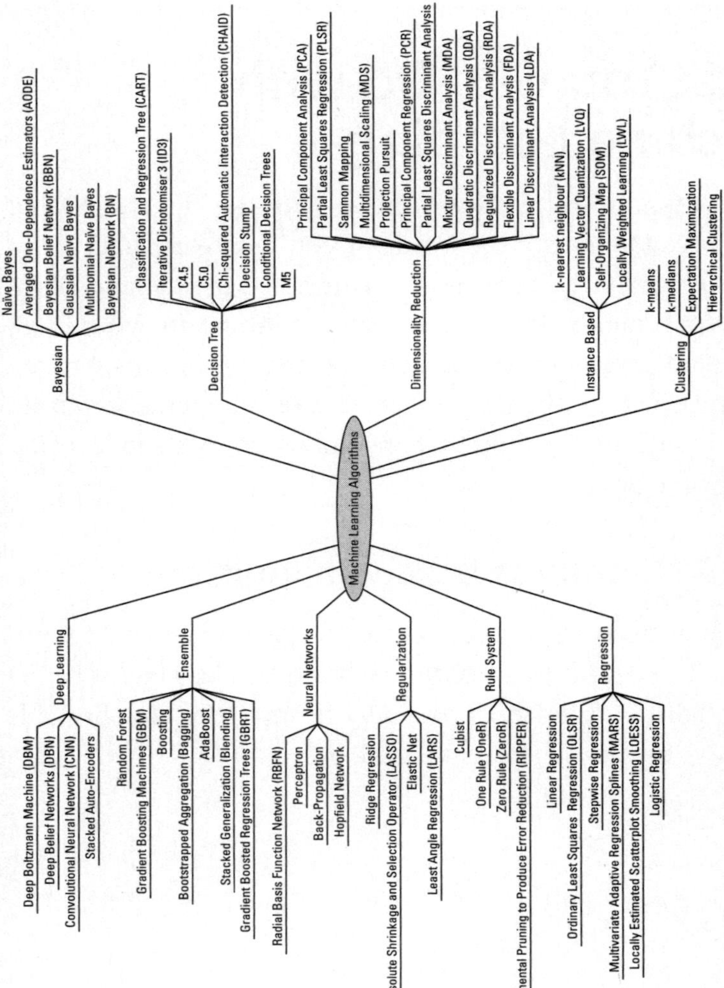

Figure 6-2: *Machine learning algorithms can be broken down by function.*

Regression algorithm

You can use this type of algorithm to model relationships between features in a dataset. You can read more on linear and logistic regression methods in Chapter 7.

Association rule learning algorithm

This type of algorithm is a rule-based set of methods that you can use to discover associations between features in a dataset.

Instance-based algorithm

If you want to use observations in your dataset to classify new observations based on similarity, you can use this type. To model with instances, you can use methods like k-nearest neighbor classification, covered in Chapter 9.

Regularizing algorithm

You can use regularization to introduce added information as a means of preventing model overfitting or to solve an ill-posed problem.

Naïve Bayes method

If you want to predict the likelihood of an event occurring based on some evidence in your data, you can use this method, based on classification and regression. Naïve Bayes is covered in Chapter 7.

Decision tree

A tree structure is useful as a decision-support tool. You can use it to build models that predict for potential fallouts that are associated with any given decision. Decision trees are covered in Chapter 8.

Clustering algorithm

You can use this type of unsupervised machine learning method to uncover subgroups within an unlabeled dataset. Both k-means clustering and hierarchical clustering are covered in Chapter 8.

Dimension reduction method

If you're looking for a method to use as a filter to remove redundant information, noise, and outliers from your data, consider dimension reduction techniques such as factor analysis and principal component analysis.

Neural network

A neural network mimics how the brain solves problems, by using a layer of interconnected neural units as a means by which to learn, and infer rules, from observational data. It's often used in image recognition and computer vision applications.

Imagine that you're deciding whether you should go to the beach. You never go to the beach if it's raining, and you don't like going if it's cooler than 75 degrees (Fahrenheit) outside. These are the two inputs for your decision. Your preference to not go to the beach when it's raining is a lot stronger than your preference to not go to the beach when it's cooler than 75 degrees, so you weight these two inputs accordingly. For any given instance where you decide whether you're going to the beach, you consider these two criteria, add up the result, and then decide whether to go. If you decide to go, your decision threshold has been satisfied. If you decide not to go, your decision threshold was not satisfied. This is a simplistic analogy for how neural networks work.

Now, for a more technical definition. The simplest type of neural network is the *Perceptron*. It accepts more than one input, weights them, adds them up on a processor layer, and then, based on the activation function and the threshold you set for it, outputs a result. An *activation function* is a mathematical function that transforms inputs into an output signal. The processor layer is called a *hidden layer.* A *neural network* is a layer of connected Perceptrons that all work together as a unit to accept inputs and return outputs that signal whether some criteria is met. A key feature of neural nets is that they are *self-learning* — in other words, they adapt, learn, and optimize per changes in input data. Figure 6-3 is a schematic layout that depicts how a Perceptron is structured.

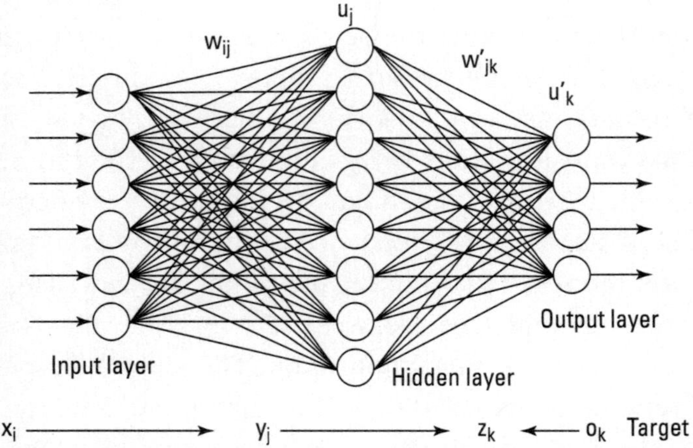

Figure 6-3: *Neural networks are connected layers of artificial neural units.*

Deep learning method

This method incorporates traditional neural networks in successive layers to offer deep-layer training for generating predictive outputs.

If you use Gmail, you probably appreciate its autoreply functionality. You know — the three 1-line messages from which you can choose an autoreply to a message someone sent you. This autoreply functionality within Gmail is called SmartReply, and it is built on deep learning algorithms. Another innovation built on deep learning is Facebook's DeepFace, the feature that automatically recognizes and suggests tags for the people who appear in your Facebook photos. Figure 6-4 is a schematic layout that depicts how a deep learning network is structured.

Deep learning is a machine learning method that uses hierarchical neural networks to learn from data in an iterative and adaptive manner. It's an ideal approach for learning patterns from unlabeled and unstructured data. It's essentially the same concept as the neural network, except that deep learning algorithms have two or more hidden layers. In fact, computer vision applications have been known to implement more than

150 hidden layers in a single deep neural network. The more hidden layers there are, the more complex a decision the algorithm can make.

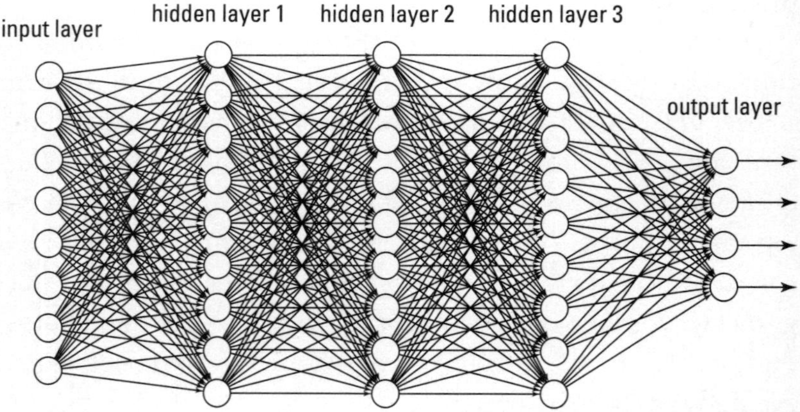

Figure 6-4: *A deep learning network is a neural network with more than one hidden layer.*

Ensemble algorithm

You can use ensemble algorithms to combine machine learning approaches to achieve results that are better than would be available from any single machine learning method on its own.

Use Spark to generate real-time big-data analytics

Apache Spark is an in-memory distributed computing application that you can use to deploy machine learning algorithms on big-data sources in near-real-time, to generate analytics from streaming big-data sources. Because it processes data in microbatches, with 3-second cycle times, you can use it to significantly decrease time-to-insight in cases where time is of the essence. It sits on top of the HDFS and acts a secondary processing framework, to be used in parallel with the large-scale batch processing work that's done by MapReduce. Spark is composed of the following submodules:

- **Spark SQL:** You use this module to work with and query structured data using Spark. Within Spark, you can query data using Spark's built-in SQL package, SparkSQL. You can also query structured data using Hive, but then you'd use the HiveQL language and run the queries using the Spark processing engine.
- **GraphX:** The GraphX library is how you store and process network data from within Spark.
- **Streaming:** The Streaming module is where the big-data processing takes place. This module basically breaks a

continuously streaming data source into much smaller data streams, called *Dstreams*, or discreet data streams. Because the Dstreams are small, these batch cycles can be completed within 3 seconds, which is why it's called microbatch processing.

- **MLlib:** The MLlib submodule is where you analyze data, generate statistics, and deploy machine learning algorithms from within the Spark environment. MLlib has APIs for Java, Scala, Python, and R. The MLlib module allows you to build machine learning models in Python or R but pull data directly from the HDFS (rather than via an intermediary repository). This helps reduce the reliance that data scientists sometimes have on data engineers. Furthermore, computations are known to be 100 times faster when processed in-memory using Spark as opposed to the standard MapReduce framework.

You can deploy Spark on-premise by downloading the open-source framework from the Apache Spark website: `http://spark.apache.org/downloads.html`. Another option is to run Spark on the cloud via the Apache Databricks service: `https://databricks.com`.

7

Math, Probability, and Statistical Modeling

Contrary to what many pure statisticians would have you believe, the data analysis field is not the same as the statistics field. Data analysts have substantive knowledge in one or several fields, and they use statistics, math, coding, and strong communication skills to help them discover, understand, and communicate data insights that lie within raw datasets related to their field of expertise. Statistics is a vital component of this formula, but no more vital than the others. In this chapter, you learn about the basic ideas behind probability, correlation analysis, regression analysis, outlier detection, and time series analysis.

Explore Probability and Inferential Statistics

Probability is one of the most fundamental concepts in statistics. To even get started in making sense of your data by using statistics, you need to be able to identify something as basic as whether you're looking at *descriptive* or *inferential* statistics. You also need a firm grasp of the basics of probability distribution. The following sections cover these concepts and more.

A *statistic* is a result that's derived from performing a mathematical operation on numerical data. In general, you use statistics in decision making. There are two types of statistics:

- **Descriptive:** Descriptive statistics provide a description that illuminates some characteristic of a numerical dataset, including dataset distribution, central tendency (such as mean, min, or max), and dispersion (as in standard deviation and variance).
- **Inferential:** Rather than focus on pertinent descriptions of a dataset, inferential statistics carve out a smaller section of the dataset and attempt to deduce significant information about the larger dataset. Use this type of

statistics to get information about a real-world measure in which you're interested.

It's true that descriptive statistics describe the characteristics of a numerical dataset, but that doesn't tell you why you should care. In fact, most data analysts are interested in descriptive statistics only for what they reveal about the real-world measures they describe. For example, a descriptive statistic is often associated with a *degree of accuracy,* indicating the statistic's value as an estimate of the real-world measure.

To better understand this concept, imagine that a business owner wants to estimate the upcoming quarter's profits. The owner might take an average of the past few quarters' profits to use as an estimate of how much he'll make during the next quarter. But if the previous quarters' profits varied widely, a descriptive statistic that estimated the *variation* of this predicted profit value (the amount by which this dollar estimate could differ from the actual profits he will make) would indicate just how far off the predicted value could be from the actual one.

TIP: You can use descriptive statistics in many ways — to detect outliers, for example, or to plan for feature preprocessing requirements, or to quickly identify what features you may want, or not want, to use in an analysis.

Like descriptive statistics, inferential statistics are used to reveal something about a real-world measure. Inferential statistics do this by providing information about a small data selection, so you can use this information to infer something about the larger dataset from which it was taken. In statistics, this smaller data selection is known as a *sample,* and the larger, complete dataset from which the sample is taken is called the *population.*

If your dataset is too big to analyze in its entirety, pull a smaller sample of this dataset, analyze it, and then make inferences about the entire dataset based on what you learn from analyzing the sample. You can also use inferential statistics in situations where you simply can't afford to collect data for the entire population. In this case, you'd use the data you do have to make inferences about the population at large. At other times, you may find yourself in situations where complete information for the population is not available. In these cases, you can use inferential statistics to estimate values for the missing data based on what you learn from analyzing the data that is available.

For an inference to be valid, you must select your sample carefully so that you get a true representation of the population. Even if your sample is representative, the numbers in the sample dataset will always exhibit some *noise* — random variation, in other words — that guarantees the sample statistic is not exactly identical to its corresponding population statistic.

Probability distributions

Imagine that you've just rolled into Las Vegas and settled in at your favorite roulette table over at the Bellagio. When the roulette wheel spins off, you intuitively understand that there is an equal chance that the ball will fall into any of the slots of the cylinder on the wheel. The slot where the ball will land is totally random, and the *probability*, or likelihood, of the ball landing in any one slot over another is the same. Because the ball can land in any slot, with equal probability, there is an equal probability distribution, or a *uniform probability distribution* — the ball has an equal probability of landing in any of the slots in the cylinder.

But the slots of the roulette wheel are not all the same — the wheel has 18 black slots and 20 slots that are either red or green. Because of this arrangement, there is 18/38 probability that your ball will land in a black slot. You plan to make successive bets that the ball will land in a black slot.

Your net winnings here can be considered a *random variable,* which is a measure of a trait or value associated with an object, a person, or a place (something in the real world) that is unpredictable. Because this trait or value is unpredictable, however, doesn't mean that you know nothing about it. What's more, you can use what you do know about this thing to help you in your decision making. Here's how . . .

A *weighted average* is an average value of a measure over a very large number of data points. If you take a weighted average of your winnings (your random variable) across the probability distribution, this would yield an *expectation value* — an expected value for your net winnings over a successive number of bets. (An expectation can also be thought of as a best guess, if you had to guess.) To describe it more formally, an expectation is a weighted average of some measure associated with a random variable. If your goal is to model an unpredictable variable so that you can make data-informed decisions based on what you know about its probability in a population, you can use random variables and probability distributions to do this.

When considering the probability of an event, you must know what other events are possible. Always define the set of events as *mutually exclusive* — only one can occur at a time. (Think of the six possible results of rolling a die.) Probability has these two important characteristics:

- The probability of any single event never goes below 0.0 or exceeds 1.0.
- The probability of all events always sums to exactly 1.0.

Probability distribution is classified per these five types:

- **Discrete:** A random variable where values can be counted by groupings
- **Continuous:** A random variable that assigns probabilities to a range of value

TIP

To understand discrete and continuous distribution, think of two variables from a dataset describing cars. A "color" variable would have a discrete distribution because cars have only a limited range of colors (black, red, or blue, for example). The observations would be countable per the color grouping. A variable describing cars' miles per gallon, or mpg, would have a continuous distribution because each car could have its own separate value for mpg.

- **Normal distributions (numeric continuous):** Represented graphically by a symmetric bell-shaped curve, these distributions model phenomena that tend toward some most-likely observation (at the top of the bell in the bell curve); observations at the two extremes are less likely.
- **Binomial distributions (numeric discrete):** Model the number of successes that can occur in a certain number of attempts when only two outcomes are possible (the old heads-or-tails coin flip scenario, for example). *Binary* variables — variables that assume only one of two values — have a binomial distribution.
- **Categorical distributions (non-numeric):** Represent either non-numeric categorical variables or *ordinal variables* (a special case of numeric variable that can be grouped and ranked like a categorical variable).

Conditional probability with Naïve Bayes

You can use the *Naïve Bayes* machine learning method, which was borrowed straight from the statistics field, to predict the likelihood that an event will occur, given evidence defined in your data features — something called *conditional probability*.

Naïve Bayes, which is based on classification and regression, is especially useful if you need to classify text data.

To better illustrate this concept, consider the Spambase dataset that's available from UCI's machine learning repository (`https://archive.ics.uci.edu/ml/datasets/Spambase`). That dataset contains 4,601 records of emails and, in its last field, designates whether each email is spam. From this dataset, you can identify common characteristics among spam emails. Once you've defined common features that indicate spam email, you can build a Naïve Bayes classifier that reliably predicts whether an incoming email is spam, based on the empirical evidence supported in its content. In other words, the model predicts whether an email is spam — the *event* — based on features gathered from its content — the *evidence*.

Naïve Bayes comes in three popular versions:

- **MultinomialNB:** Use this version if your variables (categorical or continuous) describe discrete frequency counts, like word counts. This version of Naïve Bayes assumes a multinomial distribution, as is often the case with text data. It does not accept negative values.
- **BernoulliNB:** If your features are binary, you use multinomial Bernoulli Naïve Bayes to make predictions.

This version works for classifying text data, but isn't generally known to perform as well as MultinomialNB. If you want to use BernoulliNB to make predictions from continuous variables, that will work, but you first need to sub-divide them into discrete interval groupings (also known as *binning*).

- **GaussianNB:** Use this version if all predictive features are normally distributed. It's not a good option for classifying text data, but it can be a good choice if your data contains both positive and negative values (and if your features have a normal distribution, of course).

Before building a Naïve Bayes classifier, consider that the model holds an *a priori* assumption. Its predictions assume that past conditions still hold true. Predicting future values from historical ones generates incorrect results when present circumstances change.

Quantify Correlation

Many statistical and machine learning methods assume that your features are independent. To test whether they're independent, though, you need to evaluate their *correlation* —

the extent to which variables demonstrate interdependency. In this section, you get a brief introduction to Pearson correlation and Spearman's rank correlation.

TIP: Correlation is quantified per the value of a variable called *r*, which ranges between –1 and 1. The closer the r-value is to –1 or 1, the more correlation there is between two variables. If two variables have an r-value that's close to 0, it could indicate that they're independent variables.

Determine relationships with Pearson correlation

If you want to uncover dependent relationships between continuous variables in a dataset, you'd use statistics to estimate their correlation. The simplest form of correlation analysis is the Pearson correlation, which assumes that

- Your data is normally distributed.
- You have continuous, numeric variables.
- Your variables are linearly related.

Because the Pearson correlation has so many conditions, *only* use it to determine whether a relationship between two variables exists, not to rule out possible relationships. If you were to get an r-value that is close to 0, it indicates that there is no linear relationship between the variables, but a nonlinear relationship between them still could exist.

Rank variable-pairs using Spearman's rank correlation

The Spearman's rank correlation is a popular test for determining correlation between ordinal variables. By applying Spearman's rank correlation, you're converting numeric variable-pairs into ranks by calculating the strength of the relationship between variables and then ranking them per their correlation.

The Spearman's rank correlation assumes that

- Your variables are ordinal.
- Your variables are related non-linearly.
- Your data is non-normally distributed.

Regression Methods

Machine learning algorithms of the regression variety were adopted from the statistics field, to provide data analysts with a set of methods for describing and quantifying the relationships between variables in a dataset. Use regression techniques if you want to determine the strength of correlation between variables in your data. You can use regression to predict future values from historical values, but be careful: Regression methods assume a cause-and-effect relationship between variables, but present circumstances are always subject to flux. Remember that predicting future values from historical ones will generate incorrect results when present circumstances change.

Linear regression

Linear regression is a machine learning method you can use to describe and quantify the relationship between your target variable, y — the *predictant,* in statistics lingo — and the dataset features you've chosen to use as predictor variables (commonly designated as dataset X in machine learning). When you use just one variable as your predictor, linear regression is as simple as the middle school algebra formula $y = mx + b$. But you can also use linear regression to quantify correlations among several variables in a dataset — called *multiple linear regression*. Before getting too excited about using linear regression, though, make sure you've considered its limitations:

- Linear regression only works with numerical variables, not categorical ones.
- If your dataset has missing values, it will cause problems. Be sure to address your missing values before attempting to build a linear regression model.
- If your data has outliers present, your model will produce inaccurate results. Check for outliers before proceeding.
- The linear regression assumes that there is a linear relationship between dataset features and the target variable. Test to make sure this is the case, and if it's not, try using a log transformation to compensate.
- The linear regression model assumes that all features are independent of each other.
- Prediction errors, or *residuals,* should be normally distributed.

Don't forget dataset size! A good rule of thumb is that you should have at least 20 observations per predictive feature if you expect to generate reliable results using linear regression.

Logistic regression

Logistic regression is a machine learning method you can use to estimate values for a categorical target variable based on your selected features. Your target variable should be numeric and contain values that describe the target's class — or category. One interesting thing about logistic regression is that, in addition to predicting the class of observations in your target variable, it indicates the probability for each of its estimates. Though logistic regression is like linear regression, its requirements are simpler, in that

- There does not need to be a linear relationship between the features and target variable.
- Residuals don't have to be normally distributed.
- Predictive features are not required to have a normal distribution.

When deciding whether logistic regression is a good choice for you, make sure to consider the following limitations:

- Missing values should be treated or removed.
- Your target variable must be binary or ordinal.
- Predictive features should be independent of each other.

Logistic regression requires a greater number of observations than linear regression to produce a reliable result. The rule of thumb is that you should have at least 50 observations per predictive feature if you expect to generate reliable results.

Detect Outliers

Many statistical and machine learning approaches assume that there are no outliers in your data. Outlier removal is an important part of preparing your data for analysis. In this section, you see a variety of methods you can use to discover outliers in your data.

Analyze extreme values

Outliers are data points with values that are significantly different from the majority of data points comprising a variable. It is important to find and remove outliers, because, left in your data, they skew variable distribution, make variance appear falsely high, and cause a misrepresentation of intervariable correlations.

Most machine learning and statistical models assume that your data is free of outliers, so spotting and removing them is a critical part of preparing your data for analysis. Not only that, you can use outlier detection to spot anomalies that represent fraud, equipment failure, or cybersecurity attacks. In other words, outlier detection is both a data preparation method and an analytical method.

Outliers fall into three categories:

- **Point:** Point outliers are data points with anomalous values compared to the normal range of values in a feature.
- **Contextual:** Contextual outliers are data points that are anomalous only within a specific context. For example, if you are inspecting weather station data from January

in Orlando, Florida, and you see a temperature reading of 23 degrees F, this would be quite anomalous because the average temperature there is 70 degrees F in January. But consider if you were looking at data from January at a weather station in Anchorage, Alaska — a temperature reading of 23 degrees F in this context is not anomalous at all.

- **Collective:** These outliers appear nearby to one another, all having similar values that are anomalous to the majority of values in the feature.

You can detect outliers using either a univariate or multivariate approach.

Univariate analysis

Univariate outlier detection is where you look at features in your dataset and inspect them individually for anomalous values. There are two methods for doing this:

- Tukey outlier labeling
- Tukey boxplot

If you want to use Tukey outlier labeling, the trick is to see how far the minimum and maximum values are from the

25 and 75 percentiles. The distance between the *1st quartile* (at 25 percent) and the *3rd quartile* (at 75 percent) is called the *interquartile range (IQR)*, and it describes the data's spread. When you look at a variable, consider its spread, its Q1 / Q3 values, and its minimum and maximum values to decide whether the variable is suspect for outliers.

TIP Here's a good rule of thumb: $a = \text{Q1} - 1.5 \times \text{IQR}$ and $b = \text{Q3} + 1.5 \times \text{IQR}$. If your minimum value is less than *a*, or your maximum value is greater than *b*, the variable probably has outliers.

In comparison, a Tukey boxplot is a pretty easy way to spot outliers. Each boxplot has *whiskers* (lines that extend vertically from the boxes) that are set at 1.5 × IQR. Any values that lie beyond these whiskers are outliers. Figure 7-1 shows outliers as they appear within a Tukey boxplot.

Multivariate analysis

Sometimes outliers only show up within combinations of data points from disparate variables. These outliers really wreak havoc on machine learning algorithms, so it's important to detect and remove them. You can use multivariate analysis of outliers to do this. A *multivariate* approach to outlier detection involves considering two or more variables at a time and inspecting them together for outliers. There are several methods you can use, including

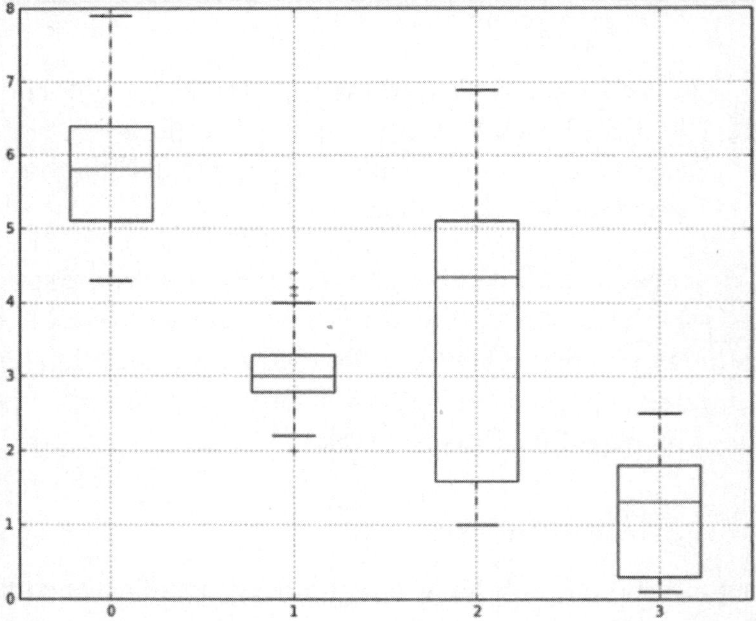

Credit: Python for DS, Lynda.com

Figure 7-1: *Spotting outliers with a Tukey boxplot.*

- Scatter-plot matrix
- Boxplot
- Density-based spatial clustering of applications with noise (DBScan)
- Principal component analysis (PCA), shown in Figure 7-2

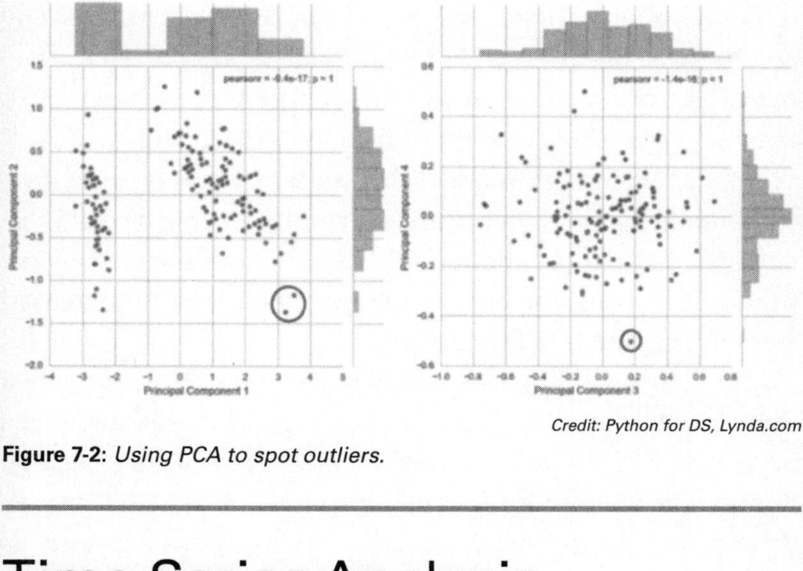

Credit: Python for DS, Lynda.com

Figure 7-2: *Using PCA to spot outliers.*

Time Series Analysis

A *time series* is a collection of data on attribute values over time. Time series analysis is performed to predict future instances of the measure based on the past observational data. To forecast or predict future values from data in your dataset, use the following two time series techniques.

Identify patterns in time series

Time series exhibit specific patterns. Take a look at Figure 7-3 to get a better understanding of what these patterns are all about. *Constant* time series remain at roughly the same level over time, but are subject to some random error. In contrast, *trended* series show a stable linear movement up or down. Whether constant or trended, time series may also sometimes exhibit *seasonality* — predictable, cyclical fluctuations that reoccur seasonally throughout a year. As an example of seasonal time series, consider how many businesses show increased sales during the holiday season.

If you're including seasonality in your model, incorporate it in the quarter, month, or even 6-month period — wherever it's appropriate. Time series may show *nonstationary processes*, that is, unpredictable cyclical behavior that is not related to seasonality and that results from economic or industry-wide conditions instead. Because they're not predictable, nonstationary processes can't be forecasted. You must transform nonstationary data to stationary data before moving forward with an evaluation.

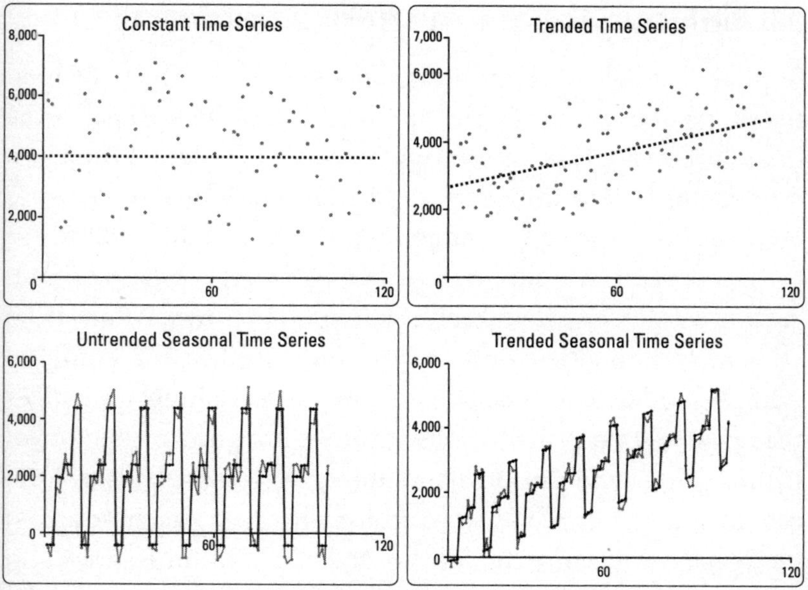

Figure 7-3: *A comparison of patterns exhibited by time series.*

Take a look at the thicker solid lines in the bottom two charts of Figure 7-3. These represent the mathematical models used to forecast points in the time series. The mathematical models shown represent very good, precise forecasts because they're a very close fit to the actual data. The actual data contains some random error, thus making it impossible to forecast perfectly.

Model univariate time series data

Similar to how multivariate analysis is the analysis of relationships between multiple variables, *univariate analysis* is the quantitative analysis of only one variable at a time. When you model univariate time series, you are modeling time series changes that represent changes in a single variable over time.

Autoregressive moving average (ARMA) is a class of forecasting methods that you can use to predict future values from current and historical data. As its name implies, the family of ARMA models combines *autoregression* techniques (analyses that assume that previous observations are good predictors of future values and perform an autoregression analysis to forecast for those future values) and *moving average* techniques — models that measure the level of the constant time series and then update the forecast model if any changes are detected. To use the ARMA model for reliable results, you need to have at least 50 observations.

If you're looking for a simple model or a model that will work for only a small dataset, the ARMA model is not a good fit for your needs. An alternative in this case might be to just stick with simple linear regression. In Figure 7-4, you can see that the model forecast data and the actual data are a very close fit.

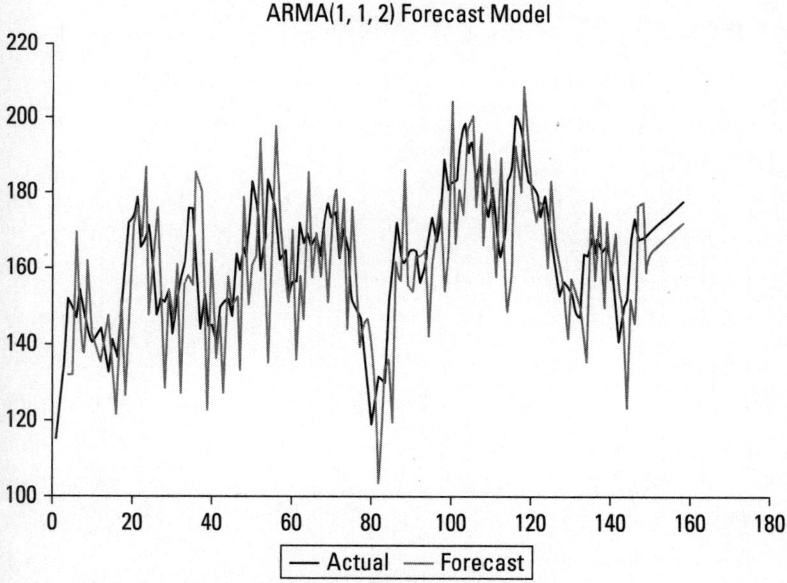

Figure 7-4: *An example of an ARMA forecast model.*

8

Subdivide Data with Clustering

Data analysts use clustering to help them divide their unlabeled data into subsets. The basics behind clustering are relatively straightforward to understand, but things get tricky fast when you get into using some of the more advanced algorithms. In this chapter, you learn the basics behind clustering. You also learn several nuanced algorithms that offer clustering solutions to meet your requirements, based on the specific characteristics of your feature dataset.

The Basics of Clustering

To grasp advanced methods for use in clustering your data, you first need to make sure you have a firm understanding of the basics that underlie all forms of clustering. *Clustering* is a form of machine learning — the *machine* in this case is your computer, and *learning* refers to an algorithm that's repeated over and over until a certain set of predetermined conditions is met. Learning algorithms are generally run until the point that the final analysis results will not change, no matter how many additional times the algorithm is passed over the data.

To put clustering through its paces, this chapter uses a readily available sample dataset from the World Bank's open datasets (see `https://data.worldbank.org`) on country income and education. This data shows the percentage of income earned by the bottom 10 percent of the population in each country and the percentage of children who complete primary school in each country.

Note that in datasets about the percentage of children who complete primary school, some are reported at over 100 percent. That's because some countries count this statistic at different ages, but the data was *normalized* so that the percentage distribution is proportionally scaled across the range of countries represented in the dataset. In other words, although the total scale exceeds 100 percent, the values have been normalized so that they're proportional to one another and you're getting an apples-to-apples comparison. Thus, the fact that some countries report completion rates greater than 100 percent has no adverse effect on the analysis you make in this chapter.

Get to know clustering algorithms

You use clustering algorithms to subdivide unlabeled datasets into clusters of observations that are most similar for a predefined feature. If you have a dataset that describes multiple features about a set of observations and you want to group your observations by their feature similarities, use clustering algorithms. There are different clustering methods, depending on how you want your dataset to be divided. The two main types of clustering algorithms are

- **Partitional:** Algorithms that create only a single set of clusters
- **Hierarchical:** Algorithms that create separate sets of nested clusters, each in its own hierarchal level

Take a look at Figure 8-1, a simple scatter plot of the Country Income and Education datasets.

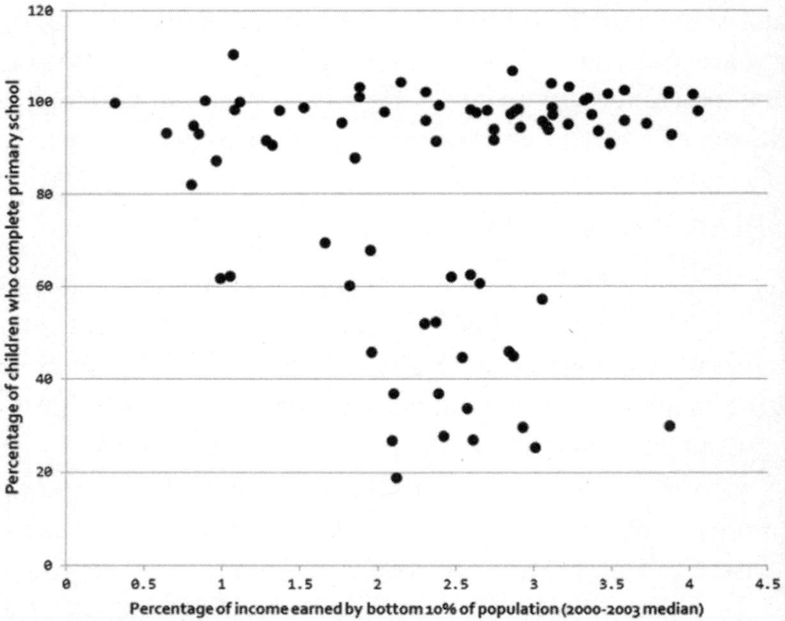

Figure 8-1: *A simple scatter plot.*

In unsupervised clustering, you start with this data and then proceed to divide it into subsets. These subsets, called *clusters,* are composed of observations that are most similar to one another. In Figure 8-1, it appears that there are at least two clusters, probably three — one at the bottom with low income and education, and then the high-education countries look like they might be split between low and high incomes.

Figure 8-2 shows the result of *eyeballing,* or making a visual estimate of clusters in this dataset.

Clustering algorithms are appropriate in situations where the following characteristics are true:

- You know and understand the dataset you're analyzing.
- Before running the clustering algorithm, you don't have an exact idea of the nature of the subsets (clusters). Often, you don't even know how many subsets are in the dataset before you run the algorithm.
- The clusters are determined by only the single dataset you're analyzing.
- Your goal is to determine a model that describes the subsets in a single dataset and only this dataset.

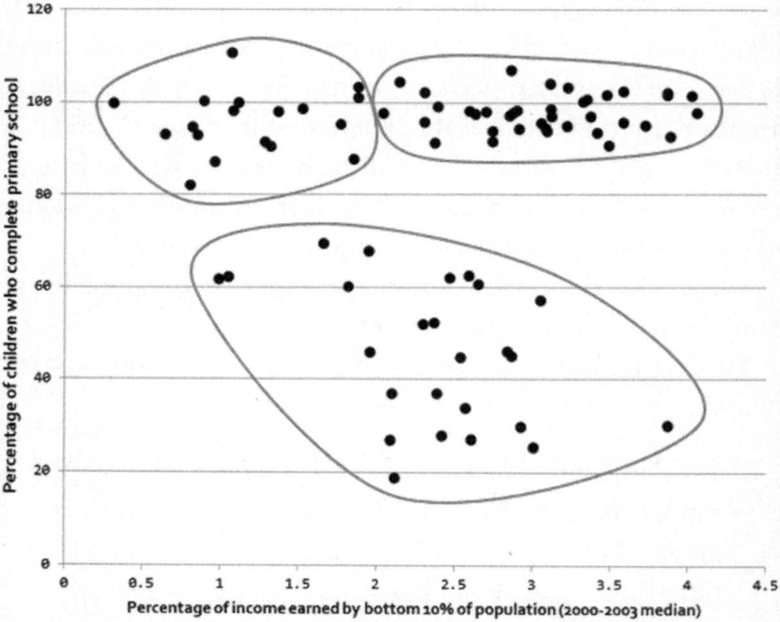

Figure 8-2: *A simple scatter plot showing eyeballed estimations of clustering.*

Clustering similarity metrics

Classification methods are based on calculating the similarity or difference between two observations. If your dataset is *numeric* — composed of only numerical features — and can be portrayed on an n-dimensional plot, you can use various geometric metrics to scale your multidimensional data. (An *n-dimensional plot* is a multidimensional scatter plot that you can use to plot *n* number of dimensions of data.)

Some popular geometric metrics used for calculating distances between observations are different geometric functions that are useful for modeling distances between points:

- **Euclidean metric:** A measure of the distance between points plotted on a Euclidean plane.
- **Manhattan metric:** A measure of the distance between points where distance is calculated as the sum of the absolute value of the differences between two points' Cartesian coordinates.
- **Minkowski distance metric:** A generalization of the Euclidean and Manhattan distance metrics. Quite often, these metrics can be used interchangeably.
- **Cosine similarity metric:** The cosine metric measures the similarity of two data points based on their orientation, as determined by taking the cosine of the angle between them.

For *non-numeric* data, you can use metrics like the *Jaccard distance metric*, an index that compares the number of features that two observations have in common. For example, to illustrate a Jaccard distance, look at these two text strings:

Saint Louis de Ha-ha, Quebec

St-Louis de Ha!Ha!, QC

What features do these text strings have in common? And what features are different between them? The Jaccard metric generates a numerical index value that quantifies the similarity between text strings.

Identify Clusters in Your Data

You can use many different algorithms for clustering, but the speed and robustness of the k-means algorithm makes it a popular choice among experienced data analysts. Kernel density estimation methods, hierarchical algorithms, and neighborhood algorithms are also available to help you identify clusters in your dataset. These alternative methods are discussed later in the chapter.

Clustering with the k-means algorithm

The *k-means* clustering algorithm is a simple, fast, unsupervised learning algorithm that you can use to predict groupings within a dataset. The model makes its prediction based on the *number of centroids present* — represented by *k*, a model parameter that you must define — and the nearest mean values, measured by the Euclidean distance between observations. Because the features of a dataset are usually on different scales, the difference of scales can distort the results of this distance calculation. To avoid this problem, scale your variables before using k-means to predict data groupings.

The quality of the clusters is heavily dependent on the correctness of the *k* value you specify. If your data is two- or three-dimensional, a plausible range of *k* values may be visually determinable. In the eyeballed approximation of clustering from the World Bank Income and Education data scatter plot (refer to Figure 8-2), a visual estimation of the *k* value would equate to three clusters, or $k = 3$.

TIP

When defining the *k* value, it may be possible to choose the number of centroids by looking at a scatter plot (if your dataset is two- or three-dimensional) or by looking for obvious, significant groupings within your dataset's variables. You can pick the number of centroids based on the number of groupings that you know exist in the dataset, or by the number of groupings that you want to exist in the dataset. Whatever the case, use your subjective knowledge about the dataset when choosing the number of clusters to be modeled.

If your dataset has more than three dimensions, however, you can use computational methods to generate a good value for *k*. One such method is the *silhouette coefficient*, which calculates the average distance of each point from all other points in a cluster and then compares that value with the average distance to every point in every other cluster. Luckily, because the k-means algorithm is efficient, it does not require much computer processing power, and you can easily calculate this coefficient for a wide range of *k* values.

The k-means algorithm works by placing sample cluster centers on an *n*-dimensional plot and then evaluating whether moving them in any single direction would result in a new center with higher *density* — with more observations closer to it, in other words. The centers are moved from regions of lower density to regions of higher density until all centers are within a region of *local maximum density* — a true center of the cluster, where each cluster gets a maximum number of points closest to its cluster center. Whenever possible, you should try to place the centers yourself, manually. If that's not possible, simply place the centers randomly and run the algorithm several times to see how often you end up with the same clusters.

One weakness of the k-means algorithm is that it may produce incorrect results by placing cluster centers in areas of *local minimum density*. This happens when centers get lost in *low-density regions* (in other words, regions of the plot that have relatively few points plotted in them) and the algorithm-driven *directional movement* (the movement that's meant to increase point density) starts to bounce and oscillate between faraway clusters. In these cases, the center gets caught in a low-density space that's located between two high-point density zones. This results in erroneous clusters based around centers that converge in areas of low, local minimum density. Ironically, this happens most often when the underlying data is very well-clustered, with tight, dense regions that are separated by wide, sparse areas.

To try things out for yourself, start clustering your data with the k-means methods by using either R's cluster package or Python's Scikit-learn library.

For more on R's cluster package, check out `http://cran.r-project.org/web/packages/cluster/cluster.pdf`.

For more on Scikit-learn, check out `http://scikit-learn.org`.

Estimate clusters with kernel density estimation (KDE)

If the k-means algorithm doesn't appeal to you, you can identify clusters in your data by using a density smoothing function instead. *Kernel density estimation* (KDE) works by placing a *kernel* — a weighting function that is useful for quantifying density — on each data point in the dataset and then summing the kernels to generate a kernel density estimate for the overall region. Areas of greater point density will sum out with greater kernel density, and areas of lower point density will sum out with less kernel density.

Because kernel smoothing methods don't rely on cluster center placement and clustering techniques to estimate clusters, they don't exhibit a risk of generating erroneous clusters by placing centers in areas of local minimum density. Where k-means algorithms generate hard-lined definitions between points in different clusters, KDE generates a plot of gradual density change between observations. For this reason, it's a helpful aid when eyeballing clusters. Figure 8-3 shows what the World Bank Income and Education scatter plot looks like after a KDE has been applied.

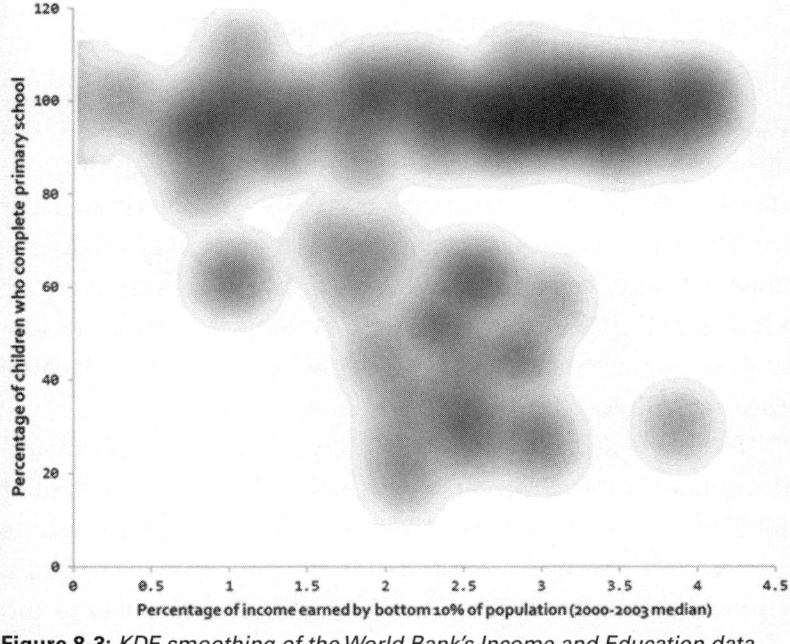

Figure 8-3: *KDE smoothing of the World Bank's Income and Education data scatter plot.*

In Figure 8-3, you can see that the white spaces between clusters have been reduced. When you look at the figure, it's fairly obvious that there are at least three clusters, and possibly more, if you want to allow for small clusters.

Cluster with hierarchical algorithms

In comparison to k-means clustering, the hierarchical clustering algorithm is a slower, clunkier unsupervised clustering algorithm. It predicts groupings within a dataset by calculating the distance and generating a link between each singular observation and its nearest neighbor. It then uses those distances to predict subgroups within a dataset. If you're carrying out a statistical study or analyzing biological or environmental data, hierarchical clustering might be your ideal machine learning solution.

To visually inspect the results of your hierarchical clustering, generate a *dendrogram* — a visualization tool that depicts the similarities and branching between groups in a data cluster. You can use several different algorithms to build a dendrogram, and the algorithm you choose dictates where and how branching occurs within the clusters. Additionally, dendrograms can be built either *bottom-up* (by assembling pairs of points and then aggregating them into larger and larger groups) or *top-down* (by starting with the full dataset and splitting it into smaller and smaller groups). Looking at the dendrogram results makes it easier to decide the appropriate number of clusters for your dataset. In the dendrogram example shown in Figure 8-4, the underlying dataset appears to have either three or four clusters.

In hierarchical clustering, the distance between observations is measured in three different ways: Euclidean, Manhattan, or Cosine. Additionally, linkage is formed by three different methods: Ward, Complete, and Average. When deciding what distance and linkage parameters to use, trial-and-error is an easy approach. Just try each combination and then compare all your model results. Go with the model that produces the most accurate prediction.

Hierarchical clustering algorithms are more computationally expensive than k-means algorithms because with each iteration of hierarchical clustering, many observations must be compared to many other observations. The benefit, however, is that hierarchical clustering algorithms are not subject to errors caused by center convergence at areas of local minimum density (as exhibited with the k-means clustering algorithms).

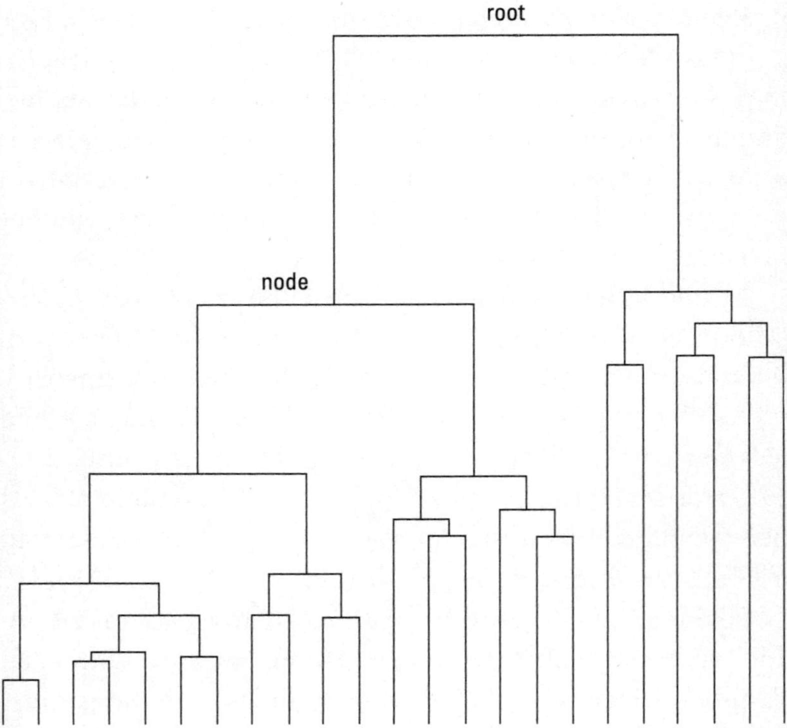

Figure 8-4: *A schematic layout of a sample dendrogram.*

A word of warning, however: If you're working with a large dataset, hierarchical clustering will probably be *way* too slow.

If you want to get started working with hierarchical clustering algorithms, check out R's hclust package or Python's Scikit-learn library. (If you're curious about hclust, go to `https://stat.ethz.ch/R-manual/R-devel/library/stats/html/hclust.html`.)

Neither k-means nor hierarchical clustering algorithms perform well when clusters are *nonglobular* — a configuration where some points in a cluster are closer to points in a different cluster than they are to points in the center of their own cluster. If your dataset shows nonglobular clustering, you can use neighborhood clustering algorithms, like DBSCAN, to determine whether each point is closer to its neighbors in the same cluster or closer to its neighboring observations in other clusters. (Figure 8-5, in the following section, shows an example of neighborhood clustering.)

Use DBSCAN

DBSCAN (density-based spatial clustering of applications with noise) is an unsupervised learning method that works by clustering *core samples* (dense areas of a dataset) while simultaneously demarking *non-core samples* (portions of the dataset that are comparatively sparse). It's a neighborhood clustering algorithm that's ideal for examining two or more variables together to identify outliers. It's particularly useful for identifying *collective* outliers — those that appear nearby to one another, all having similar values that are anomalous to most values in the variable.

Figure 8-5: *Sample output from a neighborhood clustering algorithm.*

With DBSCAN, you can take an iterative, trial-and-error approach to find the ideal number of outliers for inspection. When experimenting with the DBSCAN model, outliers should comprise 5 percent or less of the dataset's observations. You must adjust the model parameters until you've isolated this small select group of observations.

Neighborhood clustering algorithms are generally effective, but they are subject to these two weaknesses:

- **Neighborhood clustering can be computationally expensive.** With every iteration of this method, every data point might have to be compared to every other data point in the dataset.
- **With neighborhood clustering, you might have to provide the model with empirical parameter values for expected cluster size and cluster density.** If you guess either of these parameters incorrectly, the algorithm misidentifies clusters, and you must start the whole long process over again to fix the problem. If you choose to use the DBSCAN method, you're required to specify these parameters. (As an alternative, you could try the average nearest neighbor and k-nearest neighbor algorithms, which are discussed in Chapter 9.)

To avoid making poor guesses for the cluster size and cluster density parameters, you can first use a quick k-means algorithm to determine plausible values.

Categorize Data with Decision Tree and Random Forest Algorithms

In cases where clustering algorithms fail, decision tree and random forest algorithms might just offer you a perfect alternative machine learning solution. Sometimes you can get stuck trying to cluster and classify data from a non-numerical dataset. That's when you can use a decision tree model to help cluster and classify your data correctly.

A *decision tree* algorithm works by developing a set of yes-or-no rules that you can follow for new data to see exactly how it will be characterized by the model. But you must be careful when using decision tree models, because they run the high risk of *error propagation,* which occurs whenever one of the model rules is incorrect. Errors are generated in the results of decisions that are made based on that incorrect rule, and then propagated through every other subsequent decision made along that branch of the tree.

To illustrate this type of algorithm, consider a dataset that's often used in machine learning demonstrations — the list of passenger names from the *Titanic*. Using a simple decision tree model, you can predict that if a passenger was female or was a male child with a large family, he or she probably survived the catastrophe. Figure 8-6 illustrates this determination.

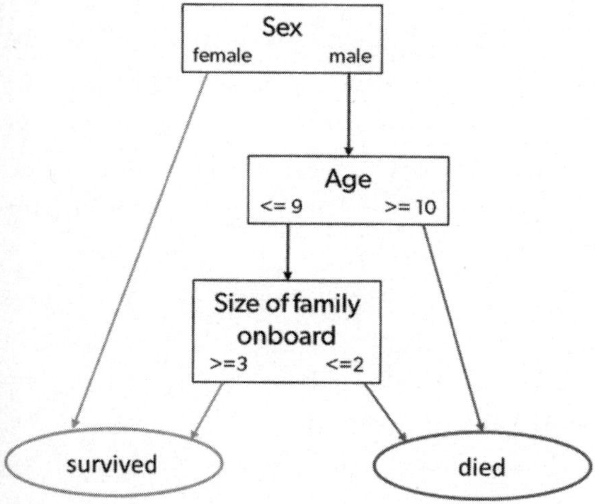

Figure 8-6: *A decision tree model predicts survival rates from the* Titanic *catastrophe.*

Random forest algorithms are a slower but more powerful alternative to the decision tree. Instead of building a tree from the data, the algorithm creates random trees and then determines which one best classifies the testing data. This method eliminates the risk of error propagation that is inherent in decision tree models.

9
Modeling with Instances

Data analysts use classification methods to help them build predictive models that they can then use to forecast the classification of future observations. Classification is a form of *supervised machine learning:* The classification algorithm learns from labeled data. Data labels make it easier for your models to make decisions based on the logic rules you've defined. Your plain-vanilla clustering algorithm, like the k-means method discussed in Chapter 8, can help you predict subgroups from within unlabeled datasets. Now it's time to take things one step further, by exploring the instance-based family of machine learning algorithms.

Instance-based learning classifiers are supervised, lazy learners — they have no training phase, and they simply memorize training data, in-memory, to predict classifications for new data points. This type of classifier looks at *instances* — observations within a dataset — and, for each new observation, the classifier searches the training data for observations that are most similar, and then classifies the new observation based on its similarity to instances in the training set. Instance-based classifiers include

- k-nearest neighbor
- Self-organizing maps
- Locally weighted learning

If you're unsure about your dataset's distribution, instance-based classifiers might be a good option, but first make sure that you know their limitations. These classifiers are not well-suited for

- Noisy data (data with unexplainable random variation)
- Datasets with unimportant or irrelevant features
- Datasets with missing values

To keep this chapter as simple as possible, you learn only about the k-nearest neighbor classification algorithm (known as kNN). The concepts involved in kNN are a bit tricky, so first you learn the simpler average nearest neighbor methods before getting into the kNN approach.

Recognize the Difference between Clustering and Classification

The purpose of both clustering and classification algorithms is to make sense of, and extract value from, large sets of structured and unstructured data. If you're working with huge volumes of unstructured data, it only makes sense to try to partition the data into some sort of logical groupings before attempting to analyze it. Both clustering and classification methods allow you to take a sweeping glance of your data en masse and then form some logical structures based on what you find there, before going deeper into the nuts-and-bolts analysis.

Clustering concepts

In their simplest form, *clusters* are sets of unlabeled data points that share similar attribute values, and *clustering algorithms* are the methods that group these data points into different clusters based on their similarities. You'll see clustering algorithms used for disease classification in medical science, but you'll also see them used for customer classification in marketing research and for environmental health risk assessment in environmental engineering.

Classification algorithms

You might have heard of classification and thought that it's the same concept as clustering. Many people do, but this is not the case. In *classification,* your data is *labeled,* so before you analyze it, you already know the number of classes into which it should be grouped. You also already know what class you want assigned to each data point. In contrast, with *clustering* methods, your data is *unlabeled,* so you have no predefined concept of how many clusters are appropriate. You must rely on the clustering algorithms to sort and cluster the data in the most appropriate way.

With classification algorithms, you use what you know about an existing labeled dataset to generate a predictive model for classifying future observations. If your goal is to use your dataset and its known subsets to build a model for predicting the categorization of future observations, you'll want to use classification algorithms. When implementing supervised classification, you already know your dataset's *labels*, which are used to subset observations into *classes*. Classification helps you see how well your data fits into the dataset's predefined classes so that you can then build a predictive model for classifying future observations.

Figure 9-1 illustrates how it looks to classify the World Bank's Income and Education datasets (see `https://data.worldbank.org`) according to the Continent feature.

In Figure 9-1, you can see that, in some cases, the subsets you might identify with a clustering technique correspond to the Continents category, but in other cases, they don't. For example, look at the lone Asian country in the middle of the African observations. That's Bhutan. You could use the data in this dataset to build a model that would predict a continent class for incoming observations. But if you introduced a data point for a new country that showed statistics similar to those of Bhutan, the new country could be categorized as being part of either the Asian continent or the African continent, depending on how you define your model.

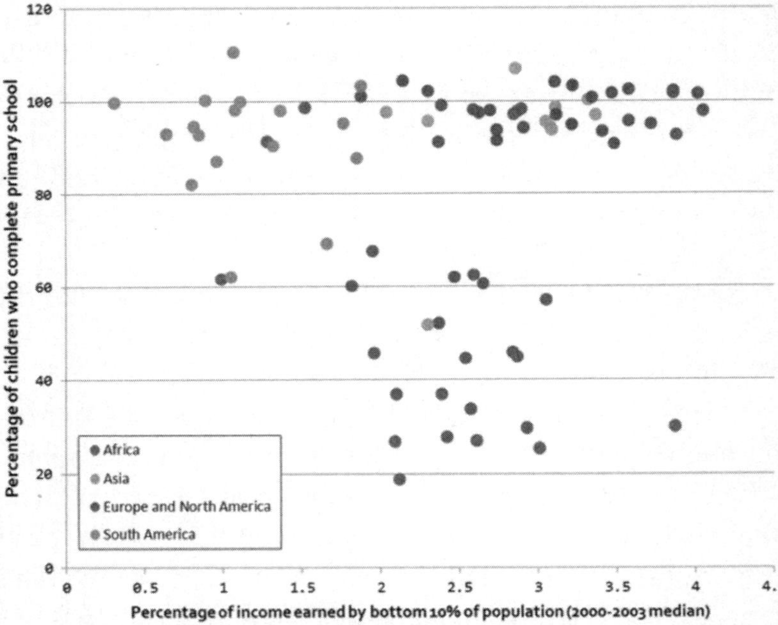

Figure 9-1: *A classification of World Bank data, according to the Continent category.*

Now imagine a situation in which your original data doesn't include Bhutan and you use the model to predict Bhutan's continent as a new data point. In this scenario, the model would incorrectly predict that Bhutan is part of the

African continent. This is an example of *model overfitting* — a situation in which a model is so tightly fit to its underlying dataset, as well as its noise or random error, that the model performs poorly as a predictor for new observations.

To avoid overfitting your models, divide your data into a training set and a test set. A typical ratio is to assign 70 percent of the data to the training set and the remaining 30 percent to the test set. Build your model with the training set, and then use the test set to evaluate the model by pretending that the test set observations are unknown. You can evaluate the accuracy of your model by comparing the classes assigned to the test set observations to the true classes of these observations.

Model overgeneralization can also be a problem. *Overgeneralization* is the opposite of overfitting: It happens when a data analyst tries to avoid misclassification due to overfitting by making a model extremely general. Models that are too general end up assigning every class a low degree of confidence. To illustrate model overgeneralization, consider again the World Bank Income and Education datasets. If the model used the presence of Bhutan to cast doubt on every new data point in its nearby vicinity, you would end up with a wishy-washy model that treats all nearby points as African, but with a low probability. This model would be a poor predictive performer.

TIP Be aware of the constant danger of overfitting and overgeneralization. Find a happy medium between the two.

When classifying data, keep these two points in mind:

- **Model predictions are only as good as the model's underlying data.** In the World Bank data example, it could be the case that, if other factors such as life expectancy or energy use per capita were added to the model, its predictive strength might increase.
- **Model predictions are only as good as the categorization of the underlying dataset.** For example, what do you do with countries, like Russia, that span two continents? Do you distinguish North Africa from sub-Saharan Africa? Do you lump North America in with Europe because they tend to share similar features? Do you consider Central America to be part of North America or South America?

Make Sense of Data with Nearest Neighbor Analysis

At their core, nearest neighbor methods work by taking an observation's attribute value and then locating another observation whose attribute value is numerically nearest to it. Because the nearest neighbor technique is a classification method, you can use it to perform tasks as scientifically oriented as deducing the molecular structure of a vital human protein or uncovering key biological evolutionary relationships, or as business-driven as designing recommendation engines for e-commerce sites or building predictive models for consumer transactions. The applications are limitless.

A good analogy for the nearest neighbor concept is illustrated in GPS technology. Imagine that you're in desperate need of a Starbucks iced latte, but you have no idea where the nearest store is located. What to do? One easy solution is simply to ask your smartphone where the nearest one is located.

When you do that, the system looks for businesses named Starbucks within a reasonable proximity of your current location.

After generating a results listing, the system reports back to you with the address of the Starbucks coffeehouse closest to your current location — the one that is your nearest neighbor, in other words.

As the term *nearest neighbor* implies, the primary purpose of a nearest neighbor analysis is to examine your dataset and find the observation that's quantitatively most similar to your observation. Note that similarity comparisons can be based on any quantitative attribute, whether that is distance, age, income, weight, or any other factor that can describe the observation you're investigating. The simplest comparative attribute is distance.

In the Starbucks analogy, the *x, y, z* coordinates of the coffeehouse reported to you by your smartphone are the most similar to the *x, y, z* coordinates of your current location. In other words, its location is closest in actual physical distance. The quantitative *attribute* being compared is distance, your current location is the *observation,* and the reported Starbucks coffeehouse is the *most similar observation*.

Keep in mind that modern nearest neighbor analyses are almost always performed using computational algorithms. The nearest neighbor algorithm is known as a *single-link algorithm* — an algorithm that merges clusters if the clusters share between them at least one *connective edge* (a shared boundary line, in other words). In the following sections, you can learn the basics of the average nearest neighbor algorithm and the k-nearest neighbor algorithm.

Classify Data with Average Nearest Neighbor Algorithms

Average nearest neighbor algorithms are basic yet powerful classification algorithms. They're useful for finding and classifying observations that are most similar on average. Average nearest neighbor algorithms are used in pattern recognition, in chemical and biological structural analysis, and in spatial data modeling. They're most often used in biology, chemistry, engineering, and geosciences.

In this section, you can find out how to use average nearest neighbor algorithms to compare multiple attributes between observations and, subsequently, identify which of your observations are most similar. You can also find out how to use average nearest neighbor algorithms to identify significant patterns in your dataset.

The purpose of using an average nearest neighbor algorithm is to classify observations based on the average of the mathematical distances between them. If your goal is to identify and group observations by average similarity, the average nearest neighbor algorithm is a great way to do that.

With respect to nearest neighbor classifiers, a dataset is composed of observations, each which has an *x*- and *y*-variable. An *x*-variable represents the input value, or *feature,* and the *y*-variable represents the data label, or target variable. To keep all these terms straight, consider the following example.

Suppose that your friendly neighborhood business analyst, Data Analyst Stu, is using average nearest neighbor algorithms to perform a classification analysis of datasets in his organization's database. He's comparing employees based on the following four features:

- Age
- Number of children
- Annual income
- Seniority

In his dataset, however (shown in Table 9-1), each employee in Stu's organization is represented by a five-dimensional *tuple* — or a set of five features:

- Employee Mike: (34, 1, 120000, 9, 0)
- Employee Liz: (42, 0, 90000, 5, 0)
- Employee Jin: (22, 0, 60000, 2, 0)
- Employee Mary: (53, 3, 180000, 30, 1)

Employee Name	Age	Number of Children	Annual Income	Seniority	Eligible to Retire
Mike	34	1	$120,000	9	0
Liz	42	0	$90,000	5	0
Jin	22	0	$60,000	2	0
Mary	53	3	$180,000	30	1

Table 9-1: *Data Analyst Stu's Employee Data.*

Using the variables Age, Number of Children, Annual Income, and Seniority as predictive features, Data Analyst Stu calculates the average mathematical distances between each of the employees. Figure 9-2 shows the calculated distances between each of the employees.

Mike	34	1	120000	9
Liz	42	0	90000	5
Distance between employees	**8**	**1**	**30000**	**4**
Mike	34	1	120000	9
Jin	22	0	60000	2
Distance between employees	**12**	**1**	**60000**	**7**
Mike	34	1	120000	9
Mary	53	3	180000	30
Distance between employees	**19**	**2**	**60000**	**21**
Liz	42	0	90000	5
Jin	22	0	60000	2
Distance between employees	**20**	**0**	**30000**	**3**
Liz	42	0	90000	5
Mary	53	3	180000	30
Distance between employees	**11**	**3**	**90000**	**25**
Jin	22	0	60000	2
Mary	53	3	180000	30
Distance between employees	**31**	**3**	**120000**	**28**

Figure 9-2: *The distances between the employees' tuples.*

After Data Analyst Stu has this mathematical measure of distance between the employees, he finds the *average nearest neighbor* by taking an average of these separation distances. Figure 9-3 shows that average similarity.

Stu then groups the employees by the average separation distance between them. Because the average separation distance values between Mike, Liz, and Jin are the smallest, they're grouped into class 0. Mary's average separation distances are quite unlike the others, so she is put into her own class — class 1.

Finding Average Similarities	
Average Distance (Mike - Liz)	
Average Distance Value - (Average of 8, 1, 30000, 4)	7503.25
Average Distance (Mike - Jin)	
Average Distance Value - (Average of 12, 1, 60000, 7)	15005
Average Distance (Mike - Mary)	
Average Distance Value - (Average of 19, 2, 60000, 21)	15010.5
Average Distance (Liz - Jin)	
Average Distance Value - (Average of 20, 0, 30000, 3)	7505.75
Average Distance (Liz - Mary)	
Average Distance Value - (Average of 11, 3, 90000, 25)	22509.75
Average Distance (Jin - Mary)	
Average Distance Value - (Average of 31, 3, 120000, 28)	30015.5

Figure 9-3: *Finding the average similarity between employees.*

But does this make sense? Well, you're working with a labeled dataset and you can see that the attribute Eligible to Retire assumes only one of two possible values. So, yes. If the algorithm predicts two classifications within the data, that's a reasonable prediction. Furthermore, if Stu gets new incoming data points that are unlabeled with respect to a person's eligibility to retire, he could probably use this algorithm to predict for that eligibility, based on the other four features.

Classify Data with k-Nearest Neighbor Algorithms

k-nearest neighbor is a supervised machine learning classifier that uses the observations it memorizes from within a test dataset to predict classifications for new, unlabeled observations. kNN makes its predictions based on *similarity* — the more similar the training observations are to the new, incoming observations, the more likely it is that the classifier will assign them both the same class. kNN works best if your dataset is

- Low on noise
- Free of outliers
- Labeled
- Composed only of relevant selected features
- Composed of distinguishable groups

TIP: If you're working with a large dataset, you may want to avoid using kNN, because it will probably take way too long to make predictions from larger datasets.

In the larger context of machine learning, kNN is known as a *lazy* machine learning algorithm — in other words, it has little to no training phase. It simply memorizes training data and then uses that information as the basis on which to classify new observations. The goal of the kNN is to estimate the class of the query point *P* based on the classes of its k-nearest neighbors. In this way, kNN works in ways quite similar to how the human brain works.

The kNN algorithm is a generalization of the nearest neighbor algorithm. Rather than consider the nearest neighbor, you consider *k* numbers of nearest neighbors from within a dataset that contains *n* number of data points — *k* defines how many nearest neighbors will have an influence on the classification process. In kNN, the classifier classifies the query point *P* per the classification labels found in a majority of k-nearest points surrounding the query point.

kNN is a good classification method for you to use if you know little about the distribution of your dataset. What's more, if you do have a solid idea about your dataset's distribution and *feature selection criteria* — criteria for identifying and removing noise in the dataset — you can leverage this information to create significant enhancements in the algorithm's performance.

kNN is among the simplest and most easy-to-implement classification methods, yet it yields competitive results when compared to some of the more sophisticated machine learning methods. Probably because of its simplicity and the competitive results it provides, the kNN algorithm has been ranked among the top ten most influential data mining algorithms by the academic research community.

How the k-nearest neighbor algorithm works

To use kNN, you simply need to pick a query point — usually called *P* — in the sample dataset and then compute the k-nearest neighbors to that point. The query point *P* is classified with a label that's the same as the label of most k-nearest points that surround it. (Figure 9-4 gives a bird's-eye view of the process.)

Remember, k-nearest neighbors are quantified by either distance or similarity based on another quantitative attribute.

Consider the following example: A dataset is given by [1, 1, 4, 3, 5, 2, 6, 2, 4], and point *P* is equal to 5. Figure 9-4 shows how kNN would be applied to this dataset.

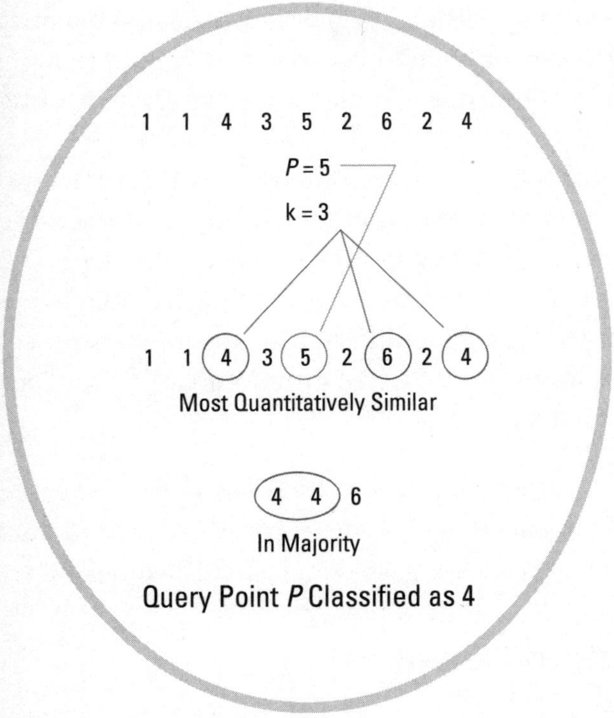

Figure 9-4: *How kNN works.*

Now, if you were to specify that *k* is equal to 3, there are, based on distance, three nearest neighbors to the point 5. Those neighbors are 4, 4, and 6. So, based on the kNN algorithm, query point *P* will be classified as 4 because 4 is the majority number in the *k* number of points nearest to it. Similarly, kNN continues defining other query points using the same majority principle.

When using kNN, it's crucial to choose a *k* value that minimizes *noise* — unexplainable random variation. At the same time, you must choose a *k* value that includes sufficient data points in the selection process. If the data points aren't uniformly distributed, it's generally harder to predetermine a good *k* value. Be careful to select an optimum *k* value for each dataset you're analyzing.

TIP

Large *k* values tend to produce less noise and more *boundary smoothing* — clearer definition and less overlap — between classes than small *k* values do.

When to use the k-nearest neighbor algorithm

kNN is particularly useful for *multi-label learning* — supervised learning where the algorithm is applied so that it automatically *learns from* (that is, detects patterns in) multiple sets of instances.

Each of these sets could potentially have several classes of their own. With multi-label learning, the algorithm learns to predict multiple class labels for each new instance it encounters.

The problem with kNN is that it takes a lot longer than other classification methods to classify a sample. Nearest neighbor classifier performance depends on calculating the distance function and on the value of the neighborhood parameter *k*. You can try to speed things up by specifying optimal values for *k* and *n*.

Common applications of k-nearest neighbor algorithms

kNN is often used for Internet database management purposes. In this capacity, kNN is useful for website categorization, webpage ranking, and other user dynamics across the web.

kNN classification techniques are also quite beneficial in *customer relationship management (CRM)*, a set of processes that ensure a business sustains improved relationships with its clients while simultaneously experiencing increased business revenues. Customer relationship management often benefits tremendously from using kNN to data-mine customer information to find patterns that are useful in boosting customer retention.

The method is so versatile that even if you're a small-business owner or a marketing department manager, you can easily use kNN to boost your own marketing return on investment. Simply use kNN to analyze your customer data for purchasing patterns, and then use those findings to customize marketing initiatives so that they're targeted toward your customer base.

Solve Real-World Problems with Nearest Neighbor Algorithms

Nearest neighbor methods are used extensively to understand and create value from patterns in retail business data. In the following sections, you see two powerful cases where k-nearest neighbor and average nearest neighbor algorithms are used to simplify management and security in daily retail operations.

k-nearest neighbor algorithms in action

K-nearest neighbor techniques for pattern recognition are often used for theft prevention in modern retail businesses. Of course, you're accustomed to seeing closed-circuit TV cameras in almost every store you visit, but most people have no idea how the data gathered from these devices is used.

You might imagine that someone in the backroom is monitoring these cameras for suspicious activity, and perhaps that is how things were done in the past. But now a modern surveillance system is intelligent enough to analyze and interpret video data on its own, without the need for human assistance. Modern systems can now use k-nearest neighbor for visual pattern recognition to scan and detect hidden packages in the bottom bin of a shopping cart at checkout. If an object is detected that is an exact match for an object listed in the database, the price of the spotted product could even automatically be added to the customer's bill. Though this automated billing practice is not used extensively now, the technology has been developed and is available for use.

K-nearest neighbor is also used in retail environments to detect patterns in credit card usage. Many new transaction-scrutinizing software applications use kNN algorithms to analyze register data and spot unusual patterns that indicate suspicious activity. For example, if register data indicates that a lot of customer information is being entered manually rather than through automated scanning and swiping, this could indicate that the employee who's using that register is in fact stealing a customer's personal information. Or, if register data indicates that a particular product is being returned or exchanged multiple times, this could indicate that employees are misusing the return policy or trying to profit from making fake returns.

Average nearest neighbor algorithms in action

Average nearest neighbor algorithm classification and point pattern detection can be used in grocery retail environments to identify key patterns in customer purchasing behavior, which can subsequently increase sales and customer satisfaction by anticipating customer behavior. Consider the following story:

As with other grocery stores, buyer behavior at (the fictional) Waldorf Food Co-op tends to follow fixed patterns. Managers have even commented on the odd fact that members of a particular age group tend to visit the store during the same particular time window, and they even tend to buy the same types of products. One day, Manager Mike got extremely proactive and decided to hire a data analyst to analyze his customer data and provide exact details about these odd trends he'd been noticing. When Data Analyst Dan got to work, he quickly uncovered a pattern among working middle-aged male adults — they tended to visit the grocery store only during the weekends or at the end of the day on weekdays, and if they came into the store on a Thursday, they almost always bought beer.

Armed with these facts, Manager Mike quickly used this information to maximize beer sales on Thursday evenings by offering discounts, bundles, and specials. Not only was the store owner happy with the increased revenues, but Waldorf Food Co-op's male customers were also happy because they got more of what they wanted, when they wanted it, at better prices.

10

The Principles of Data Visualization Design

Finding and deriving insights from raw data is at the crux of data analysis, but these insights mean nothing if you don't know how to communicate your findings to others. Data visualization is an excellent means of visually communicating the meaning of your data. To design visualizations well, however, you must know and truly understand the target audience and the core purpose for which you're designing. You must also understand the main types of data graphics that are available to you, as well as the significant benefits and drawbacks of each. In this chapter, you learn the core principles of data visualization design.

Data Visualizations: The Big Three

A *data visualization* is a visual representation that's designed for the purpose of conveying the meaning and significance of data and data insights. Since data visualizations are designed for a whole spectrum of different audiences, different purposes, and different skill levels, the first step to designing a great data visualization is to *know your audience*. Audiences come in all shapes, forms, and sizes. You could be designing for the young and edgy readers of *Rolling Stone* magazine or to convey scientific findings to a research group. Your audience might consist of board members and organizational decision-makers or a local grassroots organization.

Every audience is composed of a unique class of consumers, each with unique data visualization needs, so you must clarify for whom you're designing. This section introduces the three main types of data visualizations and then explains how to pick the one that best meets the needs of your audience.

Data storytelling for organizational decision-makers

Sometimes you must design data visualizations for a less technical-minded audience, perhaps to help members of this audience make better-informed business decisions. The purpose of this type of visualization is to tell your audience the story behind the data. In *data storytelling*, the audience depends on you to make sense of the data behind the visualization and then turn useful insights into visual stories that they can understand.

With data storytelling, your goal should be to create a clutter-free, highly focused visualization so that members of your audience can quickly extract meaning without having to make much effort. These visualizations are best delivered in the form of static images, but more adept decision-makers may prefer to have an interactive dashboard that they can use to do a bit of exploration and what-if modeling.

Data showcasing for analysts

If you're designing for a crowd of logical, calculating analysts, you can create data visualizations that are rather open-ended. The purpose of this type of visualization is to help audience members visually explore the data and draw their own conclusions.

When using *data showcasing* techniques, your goal should be to display a lot of contextual information that supports audience members in making their own interpretations. These visualizations should include more contextual data and less conclusive focus so that people can analyze the data for themselves and then draw their own conclusions. These visualizations are best delivered as static images or dynamic, interactive dashboards.

Designing data art for activists

You could be designing for an audience of idealists, dreamers, and change-makers. When designing for this audience, you want your data visualization to make a point. You can assume that typical audience members aren't overly analytical. What they may lack in math skills, however, they more than compensate for in solid convictions.

These people look to your data visualization as a vehicle by which to make a statement. When designing for this audience, *data art* is the way to go. The main goal in using data art is to entertain, provoke, annoy, or do whatever it takes to make a loud, clear, attention-demanding statement. Data art has little to no narrative and offers no room for viewers to form their own interpretations.

Whatever type of data visualization you choose, keep in mind that data analysts have an ethical responsibility to always represent data accurately. A data analyst should never distort the message of the data to fit what the audience wants to hear — not even for data art! Nontechnical audiences don't even recognize, let alone see, the possible issues. They rely on the data analyst to provide honest and accurate representations, thus amplifying the level of ethical responsibility that the data analyst must assume.

Pick the Most Appropriate Design Style

Analytical types might say that the only purpose of a data visualization is to convey numbers and facts via charts and graphs — no beauty or design is needed. But more artistic-minded folks may insist that they have to *feel* something in order to truly understand it. Truth be told, a good data visualization is neither artless and dry nor completely abstract in its artistry. Rather, its beauty and design lie somewhere between these two extremes.

To choose the most appropriate design style, you must first consider your audience (discussed earlier in this chapter) and then decide how you want them to respond to your visualization. If you're looking to entice the audience into taking a deeper, more analytical dive into the visualization, employ a design style that induces a calculating and exacting response in its viewers. But if you want your data visualization to fuel your audience's passion, use an emotionally compelling design style instead.

Induce a calculating, exacting response

If you're designing a data visualization for corporate types, engineers, scientists, or organizational decision-makers, keep the design simple and sleek, using the data showcasing or data storytelling visualization. Include a lot of bar charts, scatter plots, and line charts (see Figure 10-1). Visualizations of this style are meant to quickly and clearly communicate what's happening in the data — direct, concise, and to the point. The best data visualizations of this style convey an elegant look and feel.

Elicit a strong emotional response

If you're designing a data visualization to influence or persuade people, incorporate design artistry that invokes an emotional response in your target audience. These visualizations usually fall under the data art category, but an extremely creative data storytelling piece could also inspire this sort of strong emotional response. Emotionally provocative data visualizations often support the stance of one side of a social, political, or environmental issue. These data visualizations include fluid, artistic design elements that flow and meander, as shown in Figure 10-2. Additionally, rich, dramatic color choices can influence the emotions of the viewer. This style of data visualization leaves a lot of room for artistic creativity and experimentation.

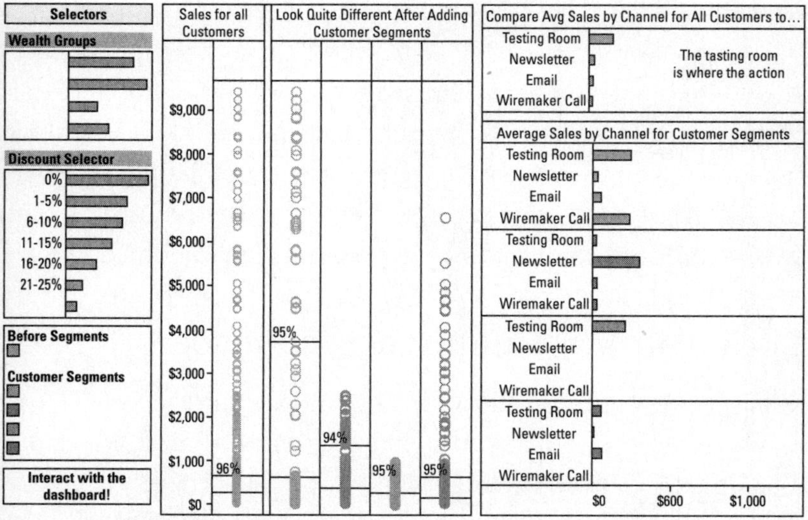

Figure 10-1: *This design style conveys a calculating and exacting feel.*

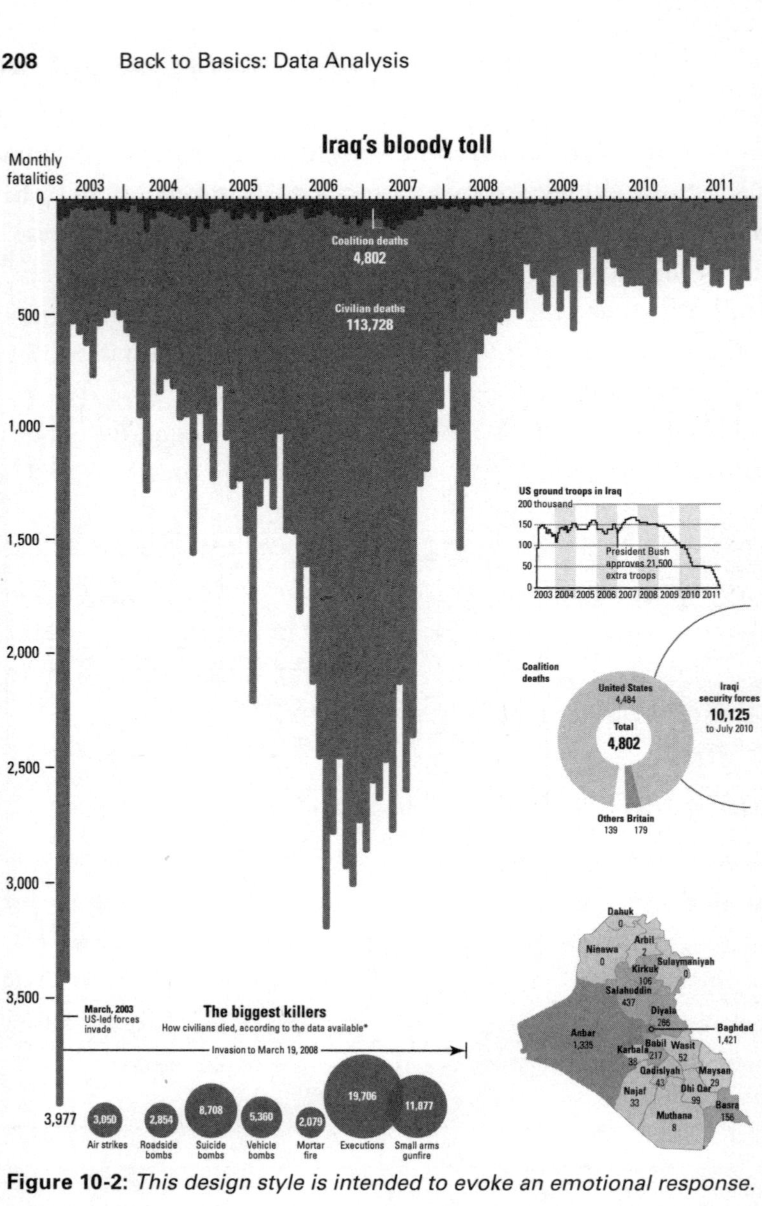

Figure 10-2: *This design style is intended to evoke an emotional response.*

TIP: Keep artistic elements relevant — and recognize when they're likely to detract from the impression you want to make, particularly when you're designing for analytical types.

Choose How to Add Context

Adding context helps people understand the value and relative significance of the information your data visualization conveys. Adding context to calculating, exacting data visualization styles helps to create a sense of relative perspective. In pure data art, you should omit context because, with data art, you're only trying to make a single point and you don't want to add information that will distract from that point.

Create context with data

In data showcasing, you should include relevant contextual data for the key metrics shown in your data visualization — for example, in a situation where you're creating a data visualization that describes conversion rates for e-commerce sales. The key metric would be represented by the percentage of users who convert to customers by making a purchase. Contextual data that's relevant to this metric might include shopping cart abandonment rates, average number of sessions before a user makes a purchase, average number of pages visited before a user makes a purchase, or specific pages that are visited before a customer decides to convert. This sort of contextual information helps viewers understand the "why and how" behind sales conversions.

Adding contextual data tends to decentralize the focus of a data visualization, so add this data only in visualizations that are intended for an analytical audience. These people are in a better position to assimilate the extra information and use it to draw their own conclusions; with other types of audiences, context is only a distraction.

Create context with annotations

Sometimes you can more appropriately create context by including annotations that provide a header and a small description of the context of the data that's shown. (See Figure 10-3.) This method of creating context is most appropriate for data storytelling or data showcasing. Good annotation is helpful to both analytical and non-analytical audiences alike.

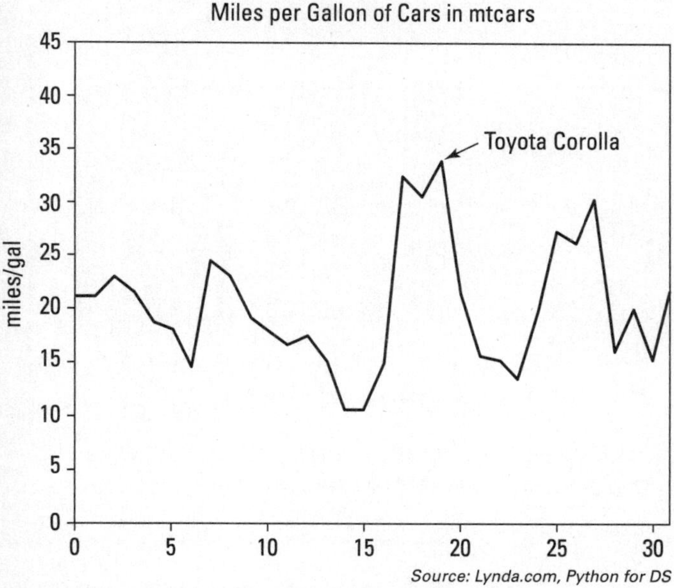

Figure 10-3: *Using annotation to create context.*

Create context with graphical elements

Another effective way to create context in a data visualization is to include graphical elements that convey the relative significance of the data. Such graphical elements include moving average trend lines, single-value alerts, target trend lines (as shown in Figure 10-4), or predictive benchmarks.

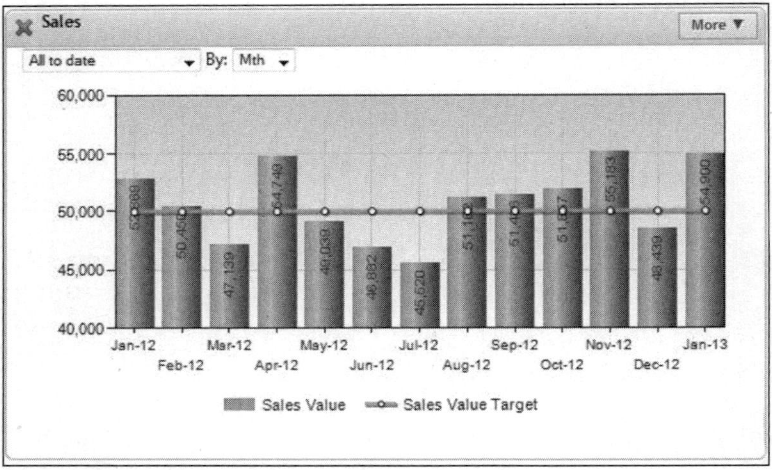

Figure 10-4: *Using graphical elements to create context.*

Select the Appropriate Data Graphic Type

Your choice of data graphic type can make or break a data visualization. Because you probably need to represent many different facets of your data, you can mix and match among the different graphical classes and types. Even among the same class, certain graphic types perform better than others; therefore, create test representations to see which graphic type conveys the clearest and most obvious message.

This chapter introduces only the most commonly used graphic types (among hundreds that are available). Don't wander too far off the beaten path. The further you stray from familiar graphics, the harder it becomes for people to understand the information you're trying to convey.

Pick the graphic type that most dramatically displays the data trends you're seeking to reveal. You can display the same data trend in many ways, but some methods deliver a visual message more effectively than others. The point is to deliver a clear, comprehensive visual message to your audience so that people can use the visualization to help them make sense of the data presented.

Among the most useful types of data graphics are standard chart graphics, comparative graphics, statistical plots, topology structures, and spatial plots and maps. The next few sections look at each type in turn.

Standard chart graphics

When making data visualizations for an audience of non-analytical people, stick to standard chart graphics. The more foreign and complex your graphics, the harder it is for non-analytical people to understand them. And not all standard chart types are boring — you have quite a variety to choose from, as the following list makes clear:

- **Area charts** (see Figure 10-5) are a fun yet simple way to visually compare and contrast attribute values. You can use them to effectively tell a visual story when you've chosen data storytelling and data showcasing.
- **Bar charts** (see Figure 10-6) are a simple way to visually compare and contrast values of parameters in the same category. Bar charts are best for data storytelling and data showcasing.
- **Line charts** (see Figure 10-7) most commonly show changes in time-series data, but they can also plot relationships between two, or even three, parameters. Line charts are versatile; you can use them in all data visualization design types.
- **Pie charts** (see Figure 10-8), which are among the most commonly used, provide a simple way to compare

values of parameters in the same category. Their simplicity, however, can be a double-edged sword; deeply analytical people tend to scoff at them, precisely because they seem so simple, so you may want to consider omitting them from data showcasing visualizations.

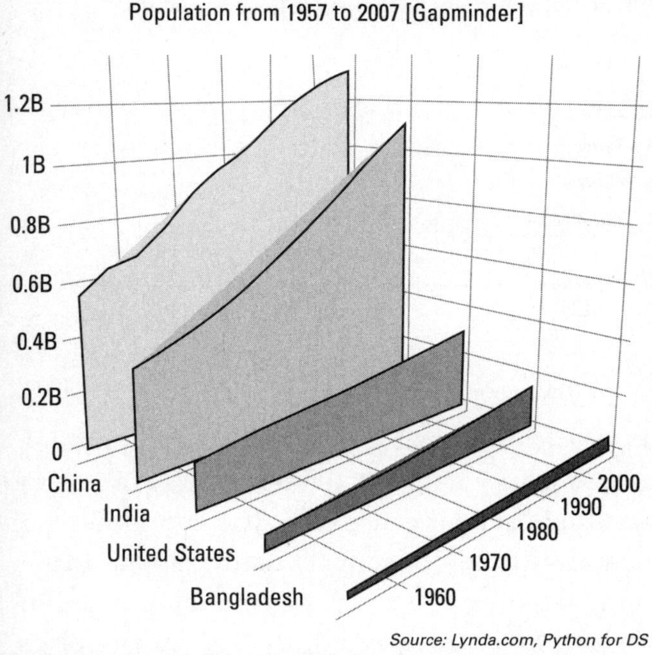

Figure 10-5: *An area chart in three dimensions.*

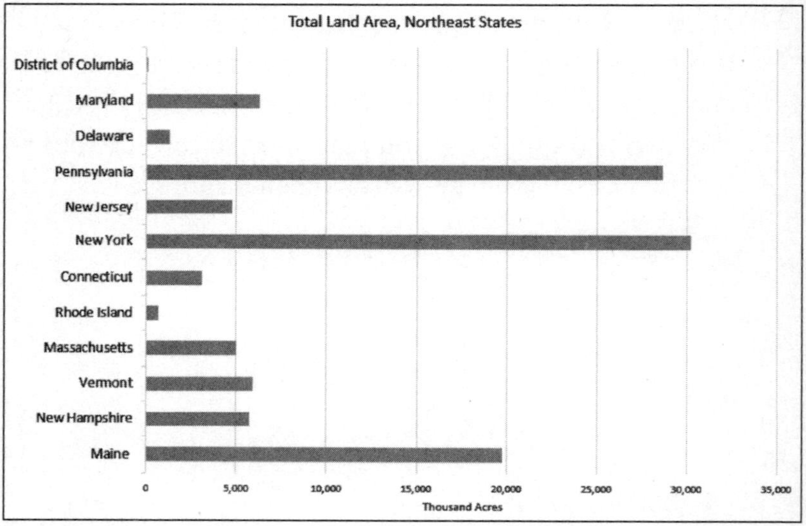

Figure 10-6: *A bar chart.*

Comparative graphics

A *comparative graphic* displays the relative value of multiple parameters in a shared category or the relatedness of parameters within multiple shared categories. The core difference between comparative graphics and standard graphics is that comparative graphics offer you a way to simultaneously compare more than one parameter and category. Standard graphics, on the other hand, provide a way to view and compare only the difference between one parameter of any single category. Comparative graphics are geared toward an audience that's at least slightly analytical, so you can easily use these graphics in either data storytelling or data showcasing. Visually speaking, comparative graphics are more complex than standard graphics.

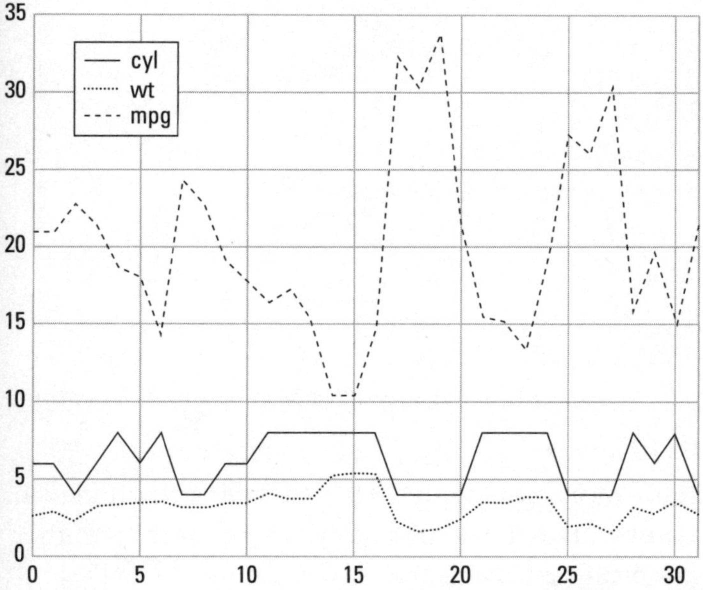

Source: Lynda.com, Python for DS

Figure 10-7: *A line chart.*

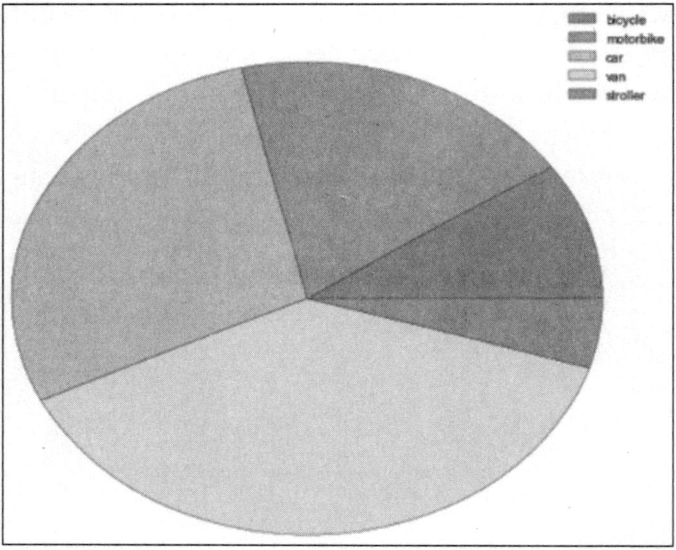

Source: Lynda.com, Python for DS

Figure 10-8: *A pie chart.*

This list shows a few different types of popular comparative graphics:

- **Bubble plots** (see Figure 10-9) use bubble size and color to demonstrate the relationship between three parameters of the same category.

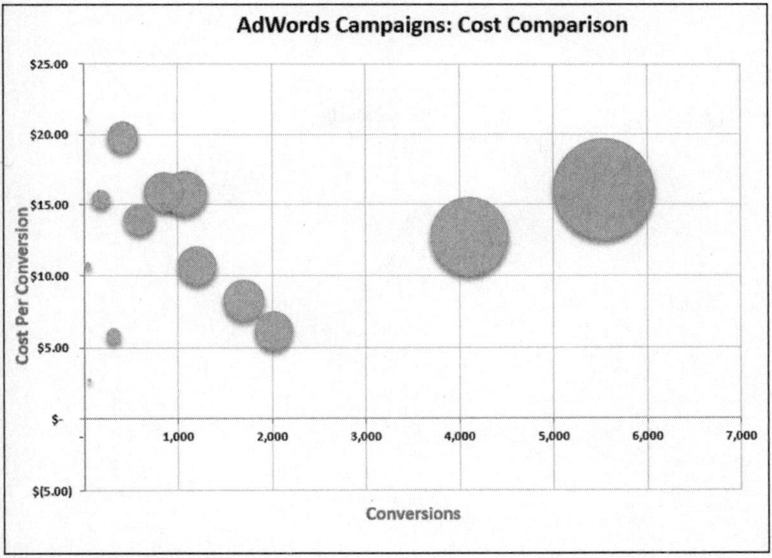

Figure 10-9: *A bubble chart.*

- **Packed circle diagrams** (see Figure 10-10) use both circle size and clustering to visualize the relationships among categories, parameters, and relative parameter values.

Figure 10-10: *A packed circle diagram.*

- **Gantt charts** (see Figure 10-11) are bar charts that use horizontal bars to visualize scheduling requirements for project management purposes. This type of chart is useful when you're developing a plan for project delivery. It's also helpful in determining the sequence in which tasks must be completed in order to meet delivery timelines.

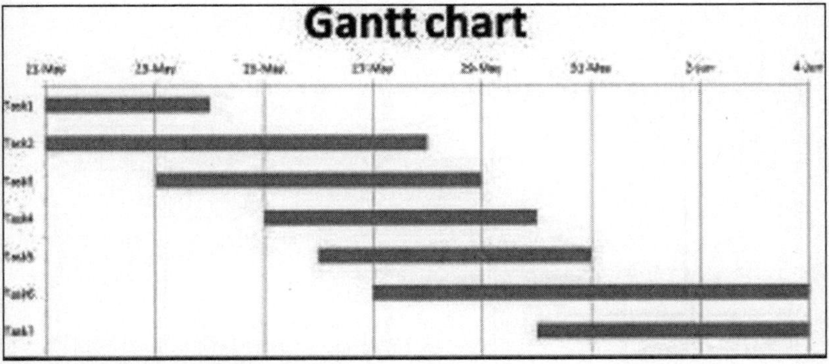

Figure 10-11: *A Gantt chart.*

- **Stacked charts** (see Figure 10-12) are used to compare multiple attributes of parameters in the same category. To ensure that it doesn't become difficult to make a visual comparison, resist the urge to include too many parameters.

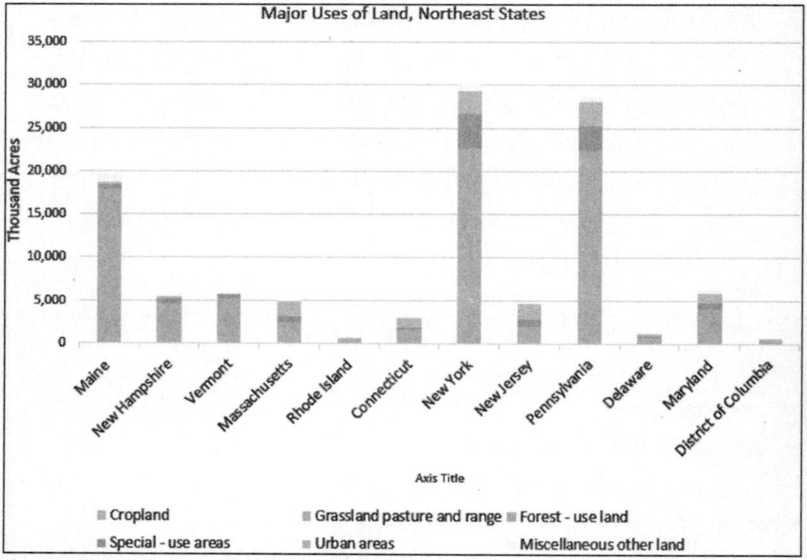

Figure 10-12: *A stacked chart.*

- **Tree maps** (see Figure 10-13) aggregate parameters of like categories and then use area to show the relative size of each category compared to the whole.
- **Word clouds** (see Figure 10-14) use type size to show the relative difference in frequency of words used in a body of text. Colors are sometimes used to indicate classifications of words by usage type.

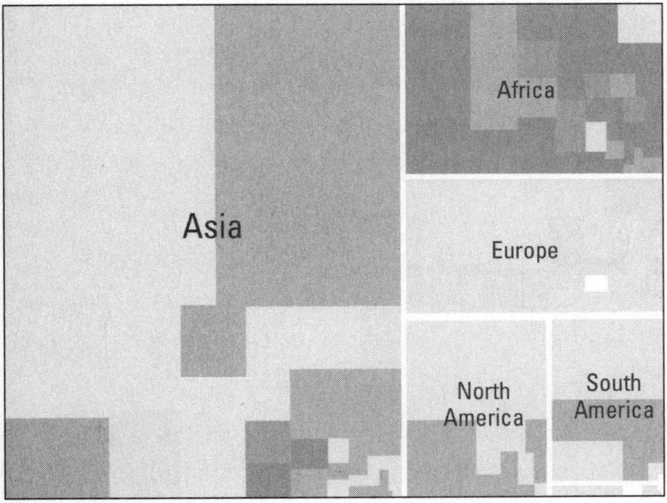

Figure 10-13: *A tree map.*

Figure 10-14: *A simple word cloud.*

Statistical plots

Statistical plots, which show the results of statistical analyses, are usually useful only to a deeply analytical audience (and aren't useful for making data art). Your statistical-plot choices are described in this list:

- **Histograms** (see Figure 10-15) are diagrams that plot a variable's frequency and distribution as rectangles on a chart. A histogram can help you quickly get a handle on the distribution and frequency of data in a dataset.

  TIP: Get comfortable with histograms. You'll see a lot of them in the course of making statistical analyses.

- **Scatter plots** (see Figure 10-16) are useful for quickly uncovering significant trends and outliers in a dataset. A scatter plot plots data points according to its *x*- and *y*-values in order to visually reveal any significant patterns. If you use data storytelling or data showcasing, start by generating a quick scatter plot to get a feel for areas in the dataset that may be interesting — areas that could potentially uncover significant relationships or yield persuasive stories.

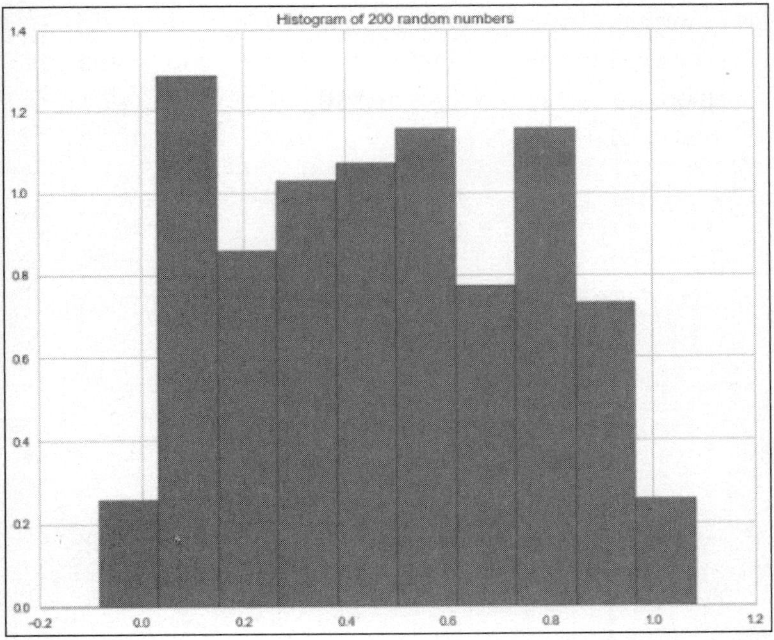

Source: Lynda.com, Python for DS

Figure 10-15: *A histogram.*

- **Scatter plot matrixes** (see Figure 10-17) are a good choice when you want to explore the relationships among several variables. A scatter plot matrix places its scatter plots in a visual series that shows correlations among multiple variables. Discovering and verifying relationships among variables can help you to identify clusters among variables and identify oddball outliers in your dataset.

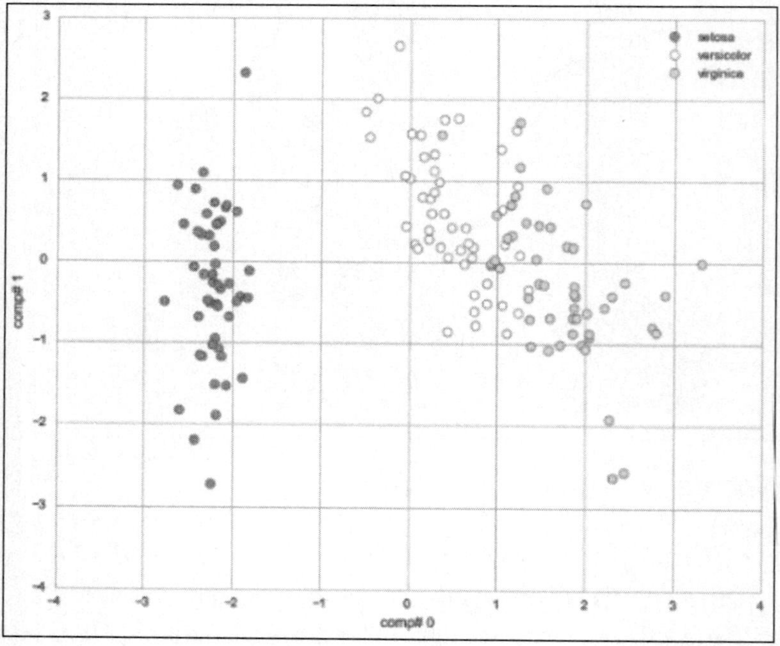

Source: Lynda.com, Python for DS

Figure 10-16: *A scatter plot.*

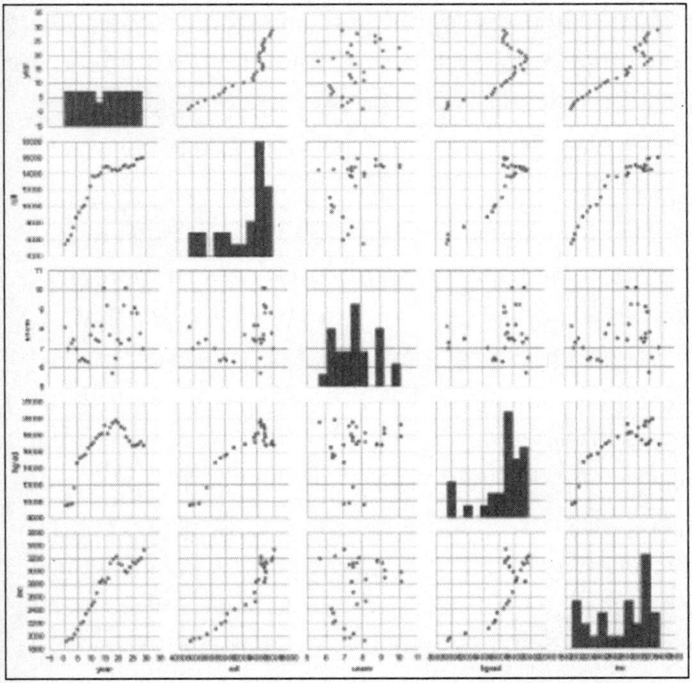

Source: Lynda.com, Python for DS

Figure 10-17: *A scatter plot matrix.*

Topology structures

Topology is the practice of using geometric structures to describe and model the relationships and connectedness between entities and variables in a dataset. You need to understand basic topology structures so that you can accurately structure your visual display to match the fundamental underlying structure of the concepts you're representing.

The following list describes a series of topological structures that are popular in data analysis:

- **Linear topological structures** (see Figure 10-18) represent a pure one-to-one relationship. Linear topological structures are often used in data visualizations that depict time-series flow patterns. Any process that can occur only by way of a sequential series of dependent events is linear, and you can effectively represent it by using this underlying topological structure.
- **Graph models** (see Figure 10-19) underlie group communication networks and traffic flow patterns. You can use graph topology to represent many-to-many relationships (as shown in the figure), such as those that form the basis of social media platforms. (In a *many-to-many* relationship structure, each variable or entity has more than one link to the other variables or entities in that same dataset.)

Figure 10-18: *A linear topology.*

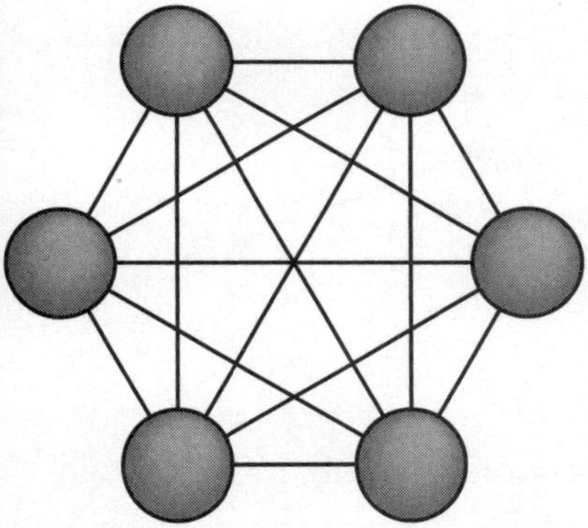

Figure 10-19: *A graph mesh network topology.*

- **Tree network topology** (see Figure 10-20) represents a *hierarchical* classification, where a network is distributed in a top-down order — nodes act as receivers and distributors of connections, and lines represent the connections between nodes. End nodes act only as receivers and not as distributors. Hierarchical classification underlies clustering and machine learning methodologies in data analysis. Tree network structures can represent one-to-many relationships, such as those that underlie a family tree or a taxonomy structure.

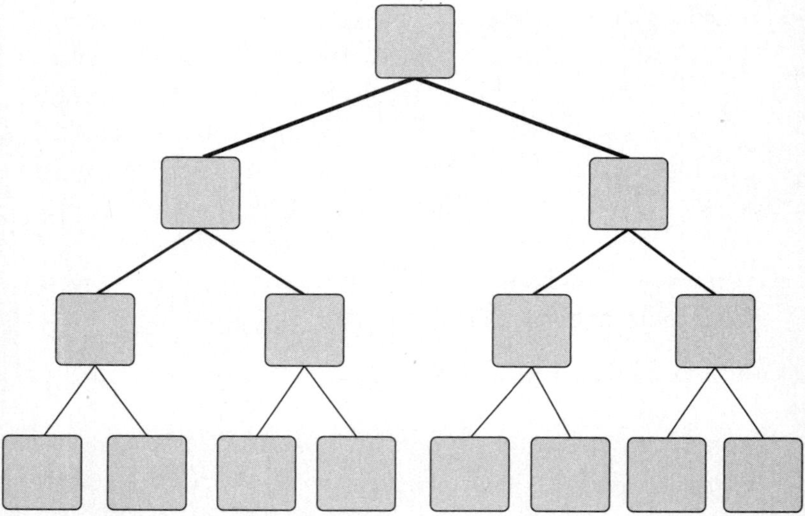

Figure 10-20: *A hierarchical tree topology.*

Spatial plots and maps

Spatial plots and maps are two different ways of visualizing spatial data. A *map* is just a plain figure that represents the location, shape, and size of features on the face of the earth. A *spatial plot,* which is visually more complex than a map, shows the values for, and location distribution of, a spatial feature's attributes.

Two types of spatial plots and maps are commonly used in data visualization:

- **Cloropleth:** Despite its fancy name, a cloropleth map is really just spatial data plotted out according to area boundary polygons rather than by point, line, or raster coverage. To better understand what this means, look at Figure 10-21. In this map, each state boundary represents an *area boundary* polygon. The color and shade of the area within each boundary represents the relative value of the attribute for that state — where red areas have a higher attribute value and blue areas have a smaller attribute value.

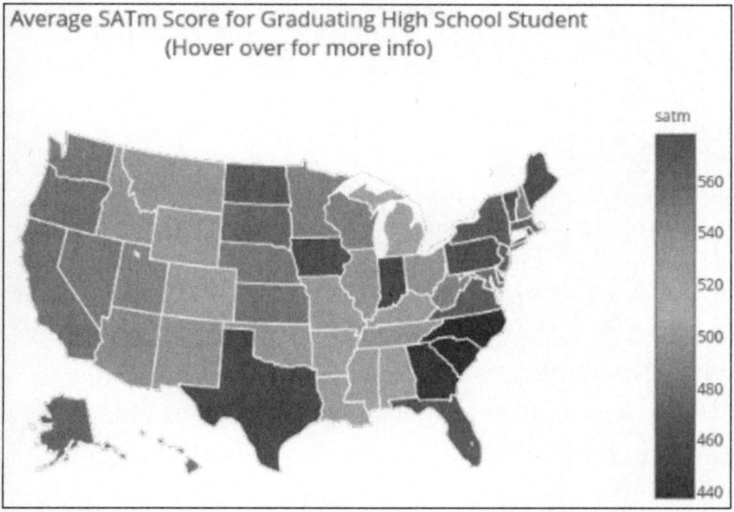

Source: Lynda.com, Python for DS

Figure 10-21: *A cloropleth map.*

- **Point:** Composed of spatial data that is plotted out according to specific point locations, a point map presents data in a graphical point form (see Figure 10-22) rather than in a polygon, line, or raster surface format.

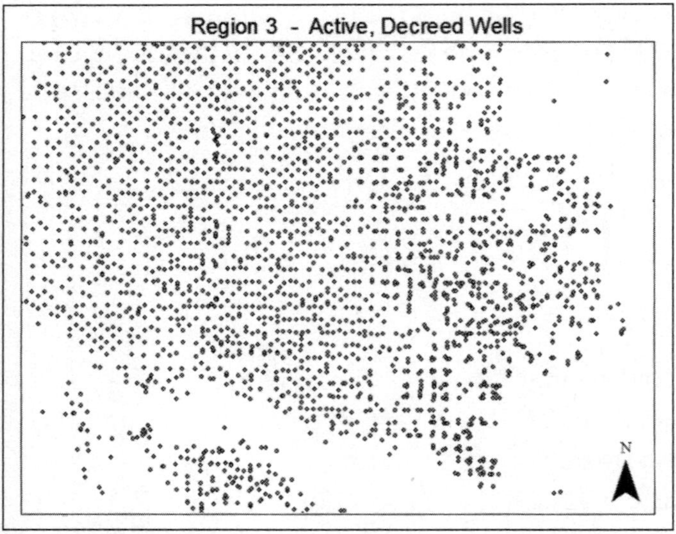

Figure 10-22: *A point map.*

11

Useful Techniques That Complement Data Analysis

There's an old saying: "When all you have is a hammer, everything looks like a nail." It's common to become so comfortable with your tools that you feel reluctant to try alternatives. You can become convinced that there's nothing your favorite tool can't do. This sort of thinking puts you at risk. It may prevent you from getting the information you need, waste your time and money, or even damage your reputation. You don't have to be an expert in every technique, of course, but a little knowledge about other tools and approaches can prepare you well for new challenges. This chapter introduces you to ten such approaches. Follow up these introductions by exploring the topics on your own.

Business Analysis

Business analysis is the study of business systems and processes with the aim of improving them. Business analysis can help organizations run more efficiently, comply with the law and other standards for good practices, and avoid costly missteps. Business analysts facilitate organizational change by identifying stakeholder needs and evaluating the feasibility of alternative solutions to business problems. Many are experts in information technology and organizational structure.

As a data analyst, your first encounter with a business analyst might come when your organization decides to explore data analysis. The business analyst might take the lead in identifying how data analysis can be applied in your organization, integrating data analysis with information technology functions, and ensuring that data analysis does not interfere with everyday operations. Later, you might support the business analyst by working with raw data to perform a data analysis relevant to a business problem that's important to the business analyst (most business analysts don't have significant skills in data analysis or statistics).

The meaning of the term *business analysis* is slippery. Confusingly, people with job titles like *business analyst*, *systems engineer*, or *systems analyst* may be true business analysts, but they are just as likely to be something else. It's not uncommon for those job titles to have other meanings. The International Institute of Business Analysts (IIBA; `www.iiba.org`) works to better define the field of business analysis and the role of the business analyst. The organization is a key resource for those who want to become, or hire, a business analyst.

Conjoint Analysis

Shoppers make choices, balancing preferences for particular features with the limitations of the products available and their shopping budget. Think about the other side of that process. If you are a product manager or marketer, to attract customers, you need information about the features they find most appealing and the prices the market will bear.

This is the role of *conjoint analysis*, a technique for obtaining information about consumer preferences. In conjoint analysis, data is collected from individuals asked to evaluate a variety of theoretical product options. These studies can vary from simple (such as those that ask respondents merely to rate or rank each option) to complex (such as studies that use special adaptive software that modifies options as the interview progresses).

Conjoint analysis is a specialized technique that calls for interactive data collection and analysis tools built specifically for this purpose. (You won't see it in data-mining applications, because the highly controlled data collection process required for conjoint analysis is quite different from the data-mining convention of using what's on hand. Some general-purpose statistical analysis tools offer conjoint analysis, but only with very limited capabilities.) Interpreting the output of these tools requires some training and practice. This training is worthwhile if you need conjoint analysis frequently, but for occasional needs, it may be better to enlist the help of a conjoint analysis specialist.

Design of Experiments

If you're a data analyst, when it comes to data, you take what you can get. Your data may be collected in the course of routine business or through another preexisting channel, but that's not always sufficient. Sometimes you need specific kinds of data, or data that fulfills certain conditions, and that's where *design of experiments* come in.

For example, say that you're investigating a problem in a manufacturing process. As a data analyst, you explore the process data on hand and look for clues to solving the problem. You might identify certain process conditions (temperature, pressure, and so on) or locations in which the problem does or does not crop up. Based on this, you come up with a theory or hypothesis — about the ideal conditions for the process, say, or the need to replace certain equipment. But you'll need more evidence to make your case.

This situation calls for a traditional statistical analysis approach. A planned experiment, one based on rigorous statistical theory, is a good choice for situations like this. The experiment may provide evidence that supports your case, or it may not. Either way, by conducting it, you avoid risk to your company's finances and to your own reputation.

If, like most data analysts, you aren't trained in the design of experiments or in strict statistical methods for analysis of the results, this is the time to bring in a statistician. A poor design can easily sink an experiment — by introducing error, for example, or by altering the meaning of the results so drastically that the experiment fails to say anything of consequence about your theory. The American Society for Quality (`https://asq.org`) is a good source for information on the design of experiments. Many of the members are experts, and the society offers classes and publishes books on this topic.

Marketing Mix Modeling

Because so many advertising options are available — TV, radio, print, online, and more — it's not always easy to figure out which combination of media provides the best value for your needs. With this in mind, marketers use *marketing mix modeling* to gain an understanding of what's working and how best to allocate their spending. Marketing mix modeling uses statistical analysis on sales and marketing data to evaluate different marketing approaches and to optimize a company's advertising choices.

Data-mining applications are not designed for marketing mix modeling. Although some methods (such as linear regression) are common to both subjects, marketing mix modeling often leans on econometric and simulation techniques that aren't typical for data analysts. For this reason, marketing mix modeling is usually done using applications designed specifically for that purpose. Although many marketers make use of marketing mix modeling, not so many are skilled at it. They often lean on consultants who are experts in these models. You should consider working with these experts, too, to fill occasional needs, or to train you if you want to do your own marketing mix modeling.

Consumer packaged goods (CPG) marketers have been using marketing mix modeling for decades, and it is now becoming popular in other industries. Competitive pressure throughout the economy is one reason. Another is U.S. Sarbanes-Oxley legislation, which requires greater controls and reporting for large expenditures by publicly traded companies.

For more information on marketing mix modeling, try the Advertising Research Foundation (`https://thearf.org`) and the Direct Marketing Association (`https://thedma.org`).

Operations Research

Consider that you have 3,000 products in 12 warehouses and 800 orders to deliver those products to customers in 14 states, using a mix of your own trucks and any of 22 supplemental delivery services, by Thursday. You must find the most cost-effective way to get everything where it needs to go, on time. For a complex problem like that, your best approach is to do *operations research.*

Operations research applies mathematical optimization, simulation, and other methods to identify ways to obtain maximum value from available resources. It's widely used in industries that have complex logistic challenges, such as transportation and the military. It's quite different from data analysis because much of the process involves no data and is based entirely on theory.

The Institute for Operations Research and the Management Sciences (`www.informs.org`), better known as *INFORMS,* and the Operational Research Society (`www.theorsociety.com`) are authoritative sources for information on operations research.

Reliability Analysis

Here's a little-known fact: Two completely different categories of analytics exist, each called *reliability analysis.* Here's the story on each of them:

- **Engineering:** In engineering, reliability analysis is exactly what the name suggests: the study of making products and their parts consistently perform as expected. It draws on mathematical modeling methods such as probabilistic risk analysis, finite element analysis, and simulation to predict how systems will function in a variety of conditions. Reliability analysis is used in manufacturing and other industries to ensure product quality and protect safety. The nuclear power industry is the most aggressive user of reliability analysis (and many of that industry's detailed risk studies are publicly available), but other manufacturers, especially manufacturers of electronics, automobiles, and toys, also use it.

  For good information on engineering reliability analysis, investigate the American Society for Quality – Reliability & Risk Division (`http://asq.org/reliability`) and the IEEE Reliability Society (`https://rs.ieee.org`).

- **Psychometrics:** In psychometrics, reliability analysis refers to consistency in a measurement. A measurement is said to be *reliable* if it produces the same result time after time.

This type of reliability analysis is most often used in the development and evaluation of standardized tests. The standardized tests used as part of the college admissions process, for example, are developed with the aid of reliability analysis. Many exams used for professional certifications also use this process.

For more about psychometric reliability analysis, touch base with the Psychometric Society (`www.psychometricsociety.org`).

Statistical Process Control

It's commonly understood that the first step to better quality is to make your processes predictable and consistent. It's a little like learning to cook something new. First you learn to make the recipe properly, and then you make small changes and see whether you can improve it.

Statistical process control formalizes that approach, using statistical measures developed for the purpose and special graphs called *control charts.* It is a longtime staple of manufacturing industries and is coming into widespread use in healthcare. Although it's also applicable to many service industry applications, it's not often used there.

Although data analysis is the product of the computer age, statistical process control originated in the days of paper and pencil computation as a means to identify and eliminate causes of variability in manufacturing processes. (That being said, most people who use statistical process control today rely on software to make their work easier.) It has its own distinctive set of charts, metrics, and ways of interpreting these to inform action, not at the executive level, but on the factory floor. Unlike data analysis, you can't perform statistical process control with data you've already collected. It requires a controlled, real-time data collection process.

The folks at the American Society for Quality (`https://asq.org`) are the experts in statistical process control. Many of the members use it every day, many are experts in the field, and pretty much all of them know a lot about it. The society offers classes and publishes books on statistical process control, too.

Social Network Analysis

Question: Which of the following is a social network?

a) Facebook

b) Pinterest

c) You, your best friend, and all your old school pals

Answer: C

Many people refer to Facebook, Pinterest, and other similar institutions as *social networks,* but in fact, these are *platforms* — that is, communication tools designed to facilitate interaction among people. The social network is the people! So you, your best friend, and all your old school pals form a social network, a group of people connected by interaction, acquaintances, or other means. *Social network analysis,* then, is the branch of mathematics that aims to understand the behavior of these interconnected groups of people.

For more information on social network analysis, try the LINKS Center for Social Network Analysis (`https://sites.google.com/site/uklinkscenter`).

Structural Equation Modeling

Human behavior is complex, involving many elements, including some that can't be directly measured. Consider the process that establishes a consumer's satisfaction level with a store. Many factors come into play: the consumer's perceived need for the store's product, the customer's attitude toward the store's atmosphere, memories of past experiences in this store and others, the weather, and so on. If you could develop a model of that process, you could understand what factors cause consumers to be satisfied or dissatisfied, and see how you might influence them to improve customer satisfaction. That's the role of *structural equation modeling* (sometimes called *path modeling* or *causative modeling*).

Structural equation modeling is well-established in academic social science research, yet few businesses have adopted it. If you have the right application, this is an opportunity to adopt a proven technique and yet be on the cutting edge in your industry. A good source for more information on structural equation modeling is the American Psychological Association (`www.apa.org`).

Web Analytics

Data analysis and other techniques designed to explore relationships among variables enable you to discover a wealth of useful information from Internet activity data. Still, this is the fancy stuff. You may have a need for some basic reports that summarize activity at a very simple level, such as tabulations of total downloads for various types of content, graphs of activity by time of day, or maybe a little bit of A/B testing (a test you can use to compare different versions of marketing materials, such as different subject lines in an email, or a red versus blue button on a webpage, and find out which works better). This is the common meaning of *web analytics*.

The place to look for information on web analytics is the Digital Analytics Association (`www.digitalanalyticsassociation.org`).

Notes

Notes

About the Authors

Meta S. Brown helps technical professionals communicate with everybody else. She's the author of *Data Mining For Dummies* and the creator of the *Storytelling for Data Analysts* and *Storytelling for Tech* workshops.

Lillian Pierson, P.E., is a leading expert in the field of big data and data science. She equips working professionals and students with the data skills they need to stay competitive in today's data-driven economy. In addition to this book, she is the author of three highly referenced technical books by Wiley: *Data Science For Dummies, Big Data / Hadoop For Dummies* (Dell Special Edition), and *Managing Big Data Workflows For Dummies* (BMC Special Edition). Lillian has spent the past decade training and consulting for large technical organizations in the private sector, such as IBM, BMC, Dell, and Intel, as well as government organizations, from the local government level all the way to the U.S. Navy. As the founder of Data-Mania LLC, Lillian offers online and face-to-face training courses as well as workshops and other educational materials in the area of big data, data science, and data analytics.

Paul McFedries is the president of Logophilia Limited, a technical writing company, and has worked with computers large and small since 1975. While now primarily a writer, Paul has worked as a programmer, consultant, database developer, and website developer. Paul has written more than 90 books that have sold over four million copies worldwide.